FROM AFRICA TO THE UNITED STATES AND THEN . . .

A Concise Afro-American History

Second Edition

FROM AFRICA
TO THE
UNITED STATES
AND THEN ...

A Concise
Afro-American
History

Second Edition

KENNETH G. GOODE
University of California, Berkeley

SCOTT, FORESMAN AND COMPANY Glenview, Illinois
Dallas, Tex.   Oakland, N.J.   Palo Alto, Ca.
Tucker, Ga.   Brighton, England

Library of Congress Cataloging in Publication Data
Goode, Kenneth G.
  From Africa to the United States and Then . . .

  Bibliography: p.
  Includes index.
  1. Afro-Americans—History. I. Title.
E185.G62 1976   973'.04'96073   75-30908
ISBN 0-673-07969-4 pbk.

1 2 3 4 5 6 7 8 9 10 -GBC- 80 79 78 77 76 75

Preface

Not many years have passed since courses and books on Afro-American history seemed to require some justification. The subject had yet to become an integral part of "American history," which tended to concern itself with a recitation of battles, elections, and the exploits of (mostly white) heroes. Since the appearance of the first edition of this book, however, awareness has steadily grown that the story of its people—black and white, native and immigrant, male and female—is the vital element of America's history.

To provide students with a point of departure from which they could begin their study of the Afro-American dimension of American history was the aim of the original edition of this volume, and remains so for this revision. It is a concise presentation of the Afro-American story, covering the main stages and developments from its origins in West Africa to the present day. It also contains extensive bibliographies, enabling students to build their knowledge through further reading. Thus, it has found a useful place as a core text for Afro-American history and Black Studies courses, as well as a supplement for the American history survey.

The continuing struggle of Afro-Americans to achieve their rightful dignity as human beings and their full rights as citizens has led to the addition of two new chapters in this second edition, covering the turbulent civil rights years and the Nixon period; the Chronological Table of Events has also been updated to include recent events. Finally, scholars in the field have continued to produce new articles and books about the Afro-American experience, and these are reflected in both the text itself and in the updated lists of readings.

Kenneth G. Goode

Table of Contents

1
West Africa

GEOGRAPHICAL BACKGROUND OF WEST AFRICA

West Africa is that part of Africa that is bounded by the Atlantic Ocean in the west and south, by the Sahara Desert in the north, and by a line corresponding approximately to Lake Chad and the present eastern boundary of Nigeria in the east. A majority of the ancestors of today's Afro-Americans came from West Africa. Large numbers also came from the Congo and Angola, but little is known about the history of these regions until the arrival of the Portuguese, who found themselves dealing with a powerful king and his "feudal" lords.

The geographical divisions in West Africa are brought about by the effect of climate, particularly rainfall. Receiving less than five inches a year on the average, the Sahara Desert supports little vegetation and a small population. In southernmost West Africa, the rainfall ranges from thirty to over one hundred inches a year. The area is covered with thick forest and abundant vegetation, and there is a comparatively dense population.

Between the Sahara Desert and the coastal forest there are various zones of vegetation. Proceeding from north to south, the Sahara Desert gives way to thorn scrub, which merges into grassland with occasional trees. The grass becomes higher and thicker and the trees larger and more numerous until they yield to the tropical coastal forest. This broad belt is known as the Western Sudan.

The coastline of West Africa offers no free natural harbors other than Dakar and Lagos. The only rivers that terminate in estuaries having any value as safe anchorages are the Gambia, Senegal, and Sierra Leone. The Bauchi Plateau in central and northern Nigeria and the Futa Jallon Plateau in southeastern West Africa are the only two areas, apart from the Cameroon Mountains in southeastern West Africa, where the level of the land rises above two thousand feet.

Until recent times, the interior of West Africa was less accessible from the Atlantic Ocean than from the north across the Sahara Desert. Travelers could cross the desert fairly easily by going from oasis to oasis. However, if they attempted to penetrate into the interior from the Atlantic Ocean, when they got ashore they were faced with the problem of traveling through tropical rain forest.

FORMATION OF SOCIETIES IN WEST AFRICA

Evidence indicates that, at the dawn of civilization, small, indigenous family groups, generally led by the oldest male, practiced a type of nomadic cultivation, which was supplemented by hunting, fishing, and gathering. These family groups lived together, found their food together, ate together, and otherwise maintained a communal type of society. With the passage of time, however, there evolved the extended family, which was composed of "relatives" (variously defined) and "slaves" (variously defined and treated).

Concidental with the evolution of the extended family group, there emerged the office of chief, to whom the group looked for leadership. The chief had an entourage, its size depending on that of the group and of the tribute received from neighboring provinces in exchange for protection. With the growth of the territory over which the chief governed, kingdoms began to emerge and the office of chief expanded to that of king.

The king was usually regarded as a sacred figure and as the dominant force in his kingdom. He wielded power through a large civil service and a powerful army. When he died, his successor generally was chosen from among members of his family. Depending on the kingdom, succession was matrilineal or patrilineal, and in a few cases succession followed the same pattern as the inheritance of property.

The king's court was made up of his immediate family, principal dignitaries, and lesser officials, and his relatives generally held the important positions at court or in outlying provinces. Also surrounding the king were eunuchs, pages, bodyguards, artisans, doctors, historians, genealogists, astrologers, and slaves.

Various methods were used to meet the expenses necessary for the upkeep of the royal house. In addition to the revenues from the royal lands, there were import and export duties, real and personal property taxes, and special levies for extraordinary circumstances.

Administration of the kingdom was very difficult, because it was virtually impossible for one person to govern a kingdom of any size. Hence, the king delegated his powers to provincial governors whose loyalty was maintained by bonds of allegiance, backed up by force. Political relations with conquered people were determined by the maintenance of military rule and the paying of tribute. The conquered people usually retained their distinctive customs and language and had little in common with their conquerors.

Every kingdom, in addition to the royal personages, had its wealthy, free citizens, skilled artisans, common laborers, serfs, and slaves. But horizontal class stratification was generally less pronounced and rigid than were the vertical barriers between family groups, clans, communities, and occupations.

West African slavery was not the chattel slavery that was to develop in America. Many "free" Africans were bound by various obligations to a lord from whom they received protection. Some "slave" Africans were given great responsibility in commercial and even political posts. Slaves often had the opportunity to become free. And free citizens could never be sure that they would not become slaves, by being captured in war or convicted of a crime. African slavery was not a rigid system separated from other social institutions. It was an integral part of the society. The slave was not an outsider but rather a lowly participant in a complex community.

Local barter was practiced within the kingdom, and trade was carried on with other kingdoms and nations, giving rise to currency. However, a single currency could not satisfy the whole of West Africa or even an individual kingdom; therefore, the need was satisfied by the use of several mediums of exchange, such as brass and iron bars.

There were varying religious concepts in West Africa that may be characterized as animistic. Some West Africans believed in a supreme being and in immortality. Some believed in many gods and in spirits of their ancestors, who dwelled in terrestrial objects and could be communicated with face to face. Many believed in a complicated theology, others were content with simpler explanations. Many embraced Islam, many refused to do so. Some kingdoms had religious ceremonies involving the sacrifice of humans, but this practice was not common.

West Africans excelled in artistic expression. Their cloth, pottery, basketry, metal, stone and ivory art pieces, implements, and weapons showed the highest skill and the keenest appreciation of beauty. Their contributions to the dance, music, and sculpture have been widely admired.

TRANS-SAHARAN TRADE

Evidence indicates that trans-Saharan trade existed as early as the days of the Carthaginians and the Roman Empire. Herodotus, in the fifth century B.C., reported that direct contact existed between the Libyan Berbers and West Africans. With the passage of time, trade reached a high level of development and organization. The trade from North Africa consisted primarily of salt, copper, and cowries. Dates, figs, coral, and implements were also imported. This merchandise was exchanged for West African gold, ivory, ebony, ostrich feathers, and slaves.

Berbers and Arabs organized the camel caravans that crossed the Sahara Desert to the commercial centers along the northern fringe of West Africa. There were three principal trade routes: (1) a western one from Morocco to the northern bend of the Niger River and to the country lying to the west of it, (2) a central route from Tunisia to the region between the bend of the Niger River and Lake Chad, and (3) an eastern route from Tripoli and Egypt to the region around Lake Chad.

NORTH AFRICAN INFLUENCE

Before the first century A.D. contact between the peoples of North Africa and West Africa was limited to periodic trade activities. But from the first century to about the thirteenth century, various political events in North Africa induced many of its people to cross the Sahara Desert and settle permanently among the West Africans. Wherever the northern immigrants settled, the character and composition of the indigenous people were affected, including their food habits, dress, architecture, language, religion, and social institutions. The impact of Islam, beginning in the ninth century, was especially important. However, without denying the profound effect northern influence had on the institutions of West Africa, such influence must not be exaggerated, for notwithstanding the different forms West African culture took, it had a common basis that never disappeared.

THE EMPIRES OF WEST AFRICA

The history of central West Africa between the fourth and eighteenth centuries is made up of a series of territorial empires, which came about as the result of (a) emigrants from North Africa imposing their rule over the West Africans, (b) indigenous groups acquiring the techniques and weapons of conquest from outsiders and successfully employing them, or (c) natural evolution.

The Empire of Ghana

The earliest of the empires was Ghana, whose evolution is distinct from other West African empires in that its foundation and early history were primarily commercial rather than military. There is controversy as to its beginnings, but there is evidence to indicate that Ghana's history goes back to the fourth century A.D. and perhaps to the pre-Christian era. It was located roughly between the Senegal and Niger Rivers, to the northwest of the modern nation of Ghana.

With the passage of time the empire grew and prospered. By the eleventh century, under the Soninke rulers, Ghana could muster an army of 200,000 troops, and its merchants carried on a lucrative trade across the Sahara Desert. The empire extended as far as Timbuctu in the east, to the upper Senegal River in the south, to the borders of Tekrur in the west, and to the southernmost Berber nomadic tribes in the Sahara Desert in the north. The greatness of Ghana stemmed from its position on the borders of the Sahara Desert and its control of a large amount of habitable territory in western West Africa. The result was that Ghana dominated the trans-Saharan trade, especially that from Morocco and Tunis.

Ghana's decline began when it was attacked from the north by the Almoravids, who were Berber tribesmen engaged in a holy war against non-Muslims. Ghana's capital fell in 1076, just ten years after England was subdued by foreign conquerors. But the Almoravids were unable to hold what they had conquered, and in 1087 Ghana regained its independence. However, the conquest disrupted the old empire, and after 1087 the authority of the kings of Ghana was effective only in a few areas. Most provinces regained their independence.

One of the provinces that broke away from Ghana after 1087 was Kaniaga. Because the So clan was prominent in aiding Kaniaga to obtain its independence, the empire became known as the Sosso Empire of Kaniaga. The Sosso struggled to erect a new empire on the chaotic ruins of old Ghana, and other states attempted the same. After several centuries of disorder a new major empire did emerge, but its nucleus was not Kaniaga but the Mandingo state of Kangaba, farther to the south and southeast.

The Empire of Mali
Kangaba, after declaring its independence from Ghana around 1087, like Kaniaga, mobilized a powerful army and began to extend its territorial borders. In extending the borders of its empire, Kangaba concentrated on areas to the south and southeast and in doing so laid the foundations of a great empire, Mali.

The success of the Mali forces incurred the hostility of the great Fulah leader, Sumanguru, to the north. As a consequence, war broke out and Mali was successful in defeating Sumanguru. Gradually Mali took over the lesser states, which were the remnants of the Ghanaian Empire. Thereafter, the goldbearing provinces to the south, which had not been a part of the Empire of Ghana, were brought into the Empire of Mali.

Reaching its peak during the early part of the fourteenth century, the empire extended from the borders of Tekrur in the west, to beyond the great bend of the Niger in the east, and from the Sahara in the north to the Futa Jallon Plateau in the south. Caravans from North Africa regularly visited Mali's commercial centers along the northern fringe of West Africa. Her ambassadors were located in every principal city in North Africa. The arts flourished, prosperity was abundant, and educational facilities were amply supported. Mali was, by contemporary European standards, an unusually large, well-governed, and unified nation.

After the death in 1332 of Mansa Musa, the greatest of its Muslim kings, the history of Mali is one of decline. Gao, a commercial and intellectual center, regained its independence. The commercial cities of Walata and Timbuctu and most of the northern part of the empire fell to the Berbers. The Woloffs and Tucolor raided with impunity from the west as did the Mossi from the south. By the middle of the fifteenth century the power of the kings of the empire extended little beyond the state of Kangaba.

The Empire of Songhay
In about 1375, the Songhay people around the city of Gao regained their

independence and founded the Songhay Empire. Gao had, in fact, been ruled by black Muslim kings for centuries and had not been long under the control of the Mali Empire. Taking advantage of the disastrous state of affairs in Mali, Songhay soon became West Africa's largest and most powerful empire. Under the brilliant administrations of Sunni Ali and Askia Muhammad, the empire was extended from the Atlantic Ocean in the west to Bornu in the east, to the upper regions of the Sahara Desert in the north, and to the Mossi states in the south.

During the reign of the great Askia Muhammad, which began in 1493, the cities of Gao, Walata, Timbuctu, and Jenne reached their peak in commercial, cultural, social, and intellectual activity. Songhay dominated all the trans-Saharan trade routes. Universities were established and those already in existence were improved. Scholars from all over the world studied and became a part of the intellectual community of Songhay. Painting and sculpture flourished, and songhay reached heights that no other West African empire had attained.

Although Askia Muhammad became blind in 1528, the Empire of Songhay continued to prosper until the latter part of that century. Songhay had one inherent weakness, however, for there was tension between Muslims in the cities and those who retained their traditional religion in the countryside. In the 1580s civil and religious wars broke out, unsuccessful military expeditions were waged, and the corrupting influence of the slave trade began to be felt.

The Sultan of Morocco, who had long sought to control the salt mines of the Sahara Desert and the gold mines of Wangara, Bambuk, and Bondu, took advantage of the situation and launched an attack against Songhay. After the loss of tens of thousands of lives, the Moroccan army defeated the forces of Songhay. They were able to do so largely because they had firearms, an unfortunate novelty in West Africa. However, because its army was small, Morocco was unable to reestablish order throughout the whole of the vast Songhay Empire. It could do little more than control the major cities of Gao, Timbuctu, and Jenne and use them as bases for punitive expeditions against rebellious provincial governors. The unified Empire of Songhay never recovered from the onslaught.

The Mossi States

One of the empires of central West Africa that retained its independence in the face of the powerful armies of Mali and Songhay and escaped the chaos that followed the Moroccan invasion was the cluster of five Mossi States. Located in the region of the Volta Basin south of the big bend of the Niger

River, the empire had been founded around the middle of the eleventh century. By the thirteenth century it was a confederation of five states—Wagadugu, Dagomba, Yatenga, Mossi, and Fada-n-Gurma. The strength of the empire lay in its efficient political and military systems. A federal government headed by a king was superimposed on the state governments. Each state had its own governor and was autonomous in local matters. The governors constituted a council, which, along with other officials, advised the king and imposed his will throughout the kingdom. The standing army was small, but its ranks could be immediately increased. (Its ability to withstand the armies of Mali and Songhay is a testimonial of this fact.)

The inhabitants of the Mossi States were primarily non-Muslim agriculturalists and itinerant traders. Their cultural, intellectual, and social attainments never reached those levels attained by other empires. Yet the Mossi States lasted longer and were more stable politically than any of the great empires of central West Africa. When they were incorporated into the French West African empire, their inhabitants were still ruled by direct descendants of the men who had created the states, and they occupied much the same territory as they had when the empire was founded.

The Kingdom of Kanem-Bornu

Prior to the ninth century, nomadic Berber tribesmen from the north and groups from the east migrated to the savannah lands north and west of Lake Chad. After the founding of the Sefuwa dynasty about 850 A.D., the rulers of Kanem began to transform the loose-knit dominion into a strong, centrally governed kingdom. By the eleventh century, strong military and political organizations had been established and commercial activities were prospering. Kanem-Bornu lay at the vital crossroads between West Africa and Egypt.

The political and military structure of Kanem was similar to those of Ghana and Mali—a powerful monarch surrounded by ministers and lesser state officials, an efficient political organization, and a large and powerful army. After the turn of the thirteenth century, a state of decline set in as the result of internal dissension among the military and the ruling house, economic setbacks, and inroads of the slave trade. The Berber Bulala of the Sahara Desert succeeded in driving the rulers of Kanem-Bornu out of the province of Kanem into Bornu where they immediately set up a new capital. After overcoming internecine quarrels during the fifteenth century, the state of Bornu grew powerful and made its influence felt in distant lands.

Bent on revenge and armed with muskets, Bornu launched an attack against the Bulala of Kanem. By 1526, Kanem was subdued and thereafter its rulers were forced to pay tribute. In the following centuries the fortunes of Kanem-Bornu fluctuated, but it was not until the nineteenth century that the Sefuwa dynasty came to an end. It had lasted a thousand years.

THE HAUSA CITY-STATES

The Hausa city-states (some of the better known were Daura, Kano, Zaria, Gobir, Katsina, and Rano) were located in the area immediately north of the point where the Niger and Benue Rivers join, in what is now Nigeria.

From the ninth or tenth centuries, the individual states vied with one another for power and influence but none was ever sufficiently powerful to control any of the others for any length of time. This lack of unity made them open to the pressures of Mali and Songhay in the east and Kanem-Bornu in the west.

Each city-state was a separate community independently governed. Cotton and grain were cultivated, and in addition the inhabitants raised livestock, wove cloth, and manufactured leather goods. But it was in the area of trade that the Hausa people made their mark. By the fifteenth century Hausa merchants were making inroads on the trade in the regions immediately north of the Gold Coast, and when the power of Songhay west of Timbuctu fell into decline, Hausa merchants came into their own. The caravan routes from Kano and Katsina to Tripoli and Tunis became the most important trans-Saharan trade routes in West Africa.

THE COASTAL FOREST KINGDOMS

The history of the coastal forest kingdoms between the fifteenth and nineteenth centuries is a series of territorial kingdoms largely resulting from commercial activities stimulated by the slave trade.

Little is known of the peoples of this area before 1000, but long before that date indigenous semi-nomadic family groups had become agriculturalists, settling down and establishing small tribal states or kingdoms occupying ill-defined areas.

The Kingdom of Benin

After many centuries of intertribal warfare, Benin emerged in the fifteenth century as the strongest and most prosperous kingdom in the coastal forest region. Many towns and villages west of the Niger River were conquered and their rulers compelled to pay tribute. The commercial activities carried on between the merchants of Benin and northern traders diminished as Benin began to trade exclusively with Europeans along the Atlantic coast. In return for slaves, pepper, ivory, and cloth, Benin imported firearms, copper, and beads. Through the seventeenth century, Benin was among the most prosperous kingdoms in the coastal forest region. Its army warred for slaves and pillaged outlying towns and villages in order to support a kingdom that stretched across the Niger delta from Bonny to Lagos and from the Atlantic Ocean far into Yorubaland.

With the passage of time, Benin found that it was increasingly difficult to obtain slaves due primarily to competition from other coastal states. This, in conjunction with other economic setbacks, inner decay, constant warfare, and the rise of the kingdom of Oyo, considerably reduced the power and influence of Benin. Thereafter, vassal states revolted and openly proclaimed their independence. By the end of the eighteenth century, its trade with foreign nations along the coast had become intermittent, its military posture weak, and its territorial size greatly diminished.

The Kingdom of Oyo

Oyo succeeded Benin as the most powerful kingdom in the coastal region. During the seventeenth century its forces subordinated peoples to both the south and north of the kingdom while its slave traders gradually ousted the merchants of Benin from their position of dominance. By the eighteenth century, Oyo, using cavalry and European-supplied arms, had established its rule over an area that extended from the borders of Benin to the western fringe of Dahomey.

Nourished by the sale of slaves, pottery, and fabrics, Oyo grew prosperous during the eighteenth century. But the very natural concentration upon the commodities that could be sold most profitably to coastal traders helped bring an end to its prosperity. The southern provinces, trading directly with the Europeans, grew wealthier than those of the north, and internal strife broke out. Toward the end of the eighteenth century, provinces within the kingdom began to proclaim their independence and inaugurated a period of civil wars that absorbed the energies of the people until they were subjected to European rule.

The Kingdom of Dahomey
The Fon people, onetime dependents of Oyo, formed the nucleus of the kingdom of Dahomey. Unlike most of the peoples on the Atlantic coastline, they organized along military rather than family lines. From their position in the transitional savannah zone just north of the coastal forest, they eyed the kingdoms on the Slave Coast, which enjoyed the benefits of a thriving trade with foreign merchants. Early in the 1720s Dahomey invaded the Slave Coast and conquered several small kingdoms.

Seeking to establish its commercial and political preeminence over the Slave Coast, to insure a steady supply of slaves, and to repel the forces of Oyo, which were constantly raiding settlements along its eastern borders, Dahomey engaged in numerous offensive and defensive military actions. Dahomey was still fighting internecine wars in an effort to maintain its commercial and political posture when the kingdom fell into European hands in the nineteenth century.

The Kingdom of Akwamu
Responding to the economic stimulus of foreign traders, coastal kingdoms west of Dahomey also began to emerge. The first was the kingdom of Akwamu, a federation of small tribal groups inhabiting the area between the Volta and Pra Rivers, in what is now the modern Republic of Ghana.

During the early seventeenth century, its rulers, taking advantage of trading of slaves and gold for guns, extended the borders of the domain to the banks of the Volta River in the east and to the Akim and Fante kingdoms in the west. After successfully subjugating the people within this area, Akwamu dominated the eastern Gold Coast and enjoyed the inherent economic advantages of its position. Aspiring to increase its territorial borders, the army of Akwamu overran more of the coast until by 1710 it controlled two hundred fifty miles of coastline.

From the rents collected from European trading posts within the kingdom, from tolls collected for the use of roads leading out of the interior to the coast, from the export and import duties placed on goods traded within the kingdom, and from the trade in slaves, Akwamu became very wealthy. However, continuous wars and severe internal strife weakened Akwamu, such that in the middle of the eighteenth century the forces of Akim were able to defeat the armies of Akwamu and reduce the kingdom to a petty principality. Thereafter, the kingdom was confined to the northwestern part of the coastal forest region in an area where the Ashanti kingdom was emerging.

The Kingdom of Ashanti

In the middle of the seventeenth century, the kingdom of Ashanti consisted of a number of small forest states located in an area west of the Volta River, in what is modern southcentral Ghana. Throughout its history, the kingdom was hindered economically by the middlemen of the coast and militarily by forces from the east. However, in the last quarter of the seventeenth century, Ashanti's ruler had the opportunity to apply the techniques of military and economic organization he had acquired while serving at the court of Akwamu. After welding the weak Ashanti states into a strong confederation, he defeated opponents in the west and south and thereby gained Ashanti's first direct contact with Europeans along the western Gold Coast.

Capitalizing on the slave trade and the rents collected from Europeans who maintained trading posts within the kingdom, Ashanti was transformed into the most powerful kingdom along the Gold Coast. Whether by trading directly with foreigners or via middlemen, the necessary supply of guns and ammunition that encouraged the development of an aggressive state was obtained. When, in the latter part of the nineteenth century, the British incorporated the kingdom into its West African empire, Ashanti was still a vital and powerful kingdom.

REFERENCES

Africanus, Joannes Leo, *The History and Description of Africa* (London: G. Bishop, 1896).

Barrows, David P., *Berbers and the Blacks; Impressions of Morocco, Timbuktu, and the Western Sudan* (New York: The Century Co., 1927).

Bovill, Edward W., *The Golden Trade of the Moors* (New York: Oxford University Press, 1958).

*Davidson, Basil, *The Lost Cities of Africa* (Boston: Atlantic Monthly Press, 1959 [ALB, Little]).

*_____, et al., *A History of West Africa to the Nineteenth Century* (New York: Doubleday, 1966 [Anchor, Doubleday]).

Delafosse, Maurice, *The Negroes of Africa: History and Culture* (Washington, D.C.: Associated Publishers, Inc., 1931).

Du Bois, W. E. B., *Black Folk, Then and Now* (New York: Henry Holt and Co., 1939).

Ellis, George W., *Negro Culture in West Africa* (New York: Neale Publishing Co., 1914).

*Fage, John D., *Introduction to the History of West Africa* (Cambridge: Cambridge University Press, 1959 [Cambridge University Press]).

*Gorer, Geoffrey, *Africa Dances: A Book About West African Negroes* (New York: Alfred A. Knopf, 1935 [W. W. Norton]).

*Herskovits, Melville J., *Myth of the Negro Past* (New York: Harper & Brothers, 1941 [Boston: Beacon Press, 1958]).

Labouret, H., *Africa Before the White Man* (New York: Walker, 1962).

Lugard, Flora L., *The Tropical Dependency* (London: James Nisbet and Co., 1905).

Stamp, Laurence Dudley, *Africa: A Study in Tropical Development* (New York: Wiley, 1953).

Sweeney, James J., *African Negro Art* (New York: Museum of Modern Art, 1925).

Trimingham, J. Spencer, *A History of Islam in West Africa* (New York: Oxford University Press, 1962).

Woodson, Carter G., *The African Background Outlined* (Washington, D.C.: Association for Study of Negro Life and History, 1936).

———, *African Heroes and Heroines* (Washington, D.C.: Associated Publishers, Inc., 1939).

*Asterisk and brackets indicate publication is in paperback form.

2
Europe and West Africa

EXPLORATION OF WEST AFRICA

From the close of the eleventh century, Europeans began to seek direct trade relations with Africa and Asia in order to obtain rare commodities such as silks and spices, which were then in very great demand. In the wake of their capture in 1415 of the North African city of Ceuta from the Moors, the Portuguese began exploring Africa's west coast. Under the sponsorship of Prince Henry the Navigator, an expedition reached Cape Verde in 1444, and by 1460, the year of Henry's death, the coast had been explored as far as Sierra Leone.

During the process of exploration, a few West Africans were taken back to Portugal to show that the adventurers had passed beyond the area of Arab domination and influence. Roman slavery had never entirely disappeared from the Iberian peninsula and some Portuguese merchants realized then that they could enrich themselves by capturing or buying West Africans, bringing them to Portugal, and selling them to work as slaves. Thus, by the middle of the fifteenth century, the European slave trade commenced.

The Portuguese were not the sole pioneers of European sea trade with West Africa. Thus on no less than three occasions, 1451, 1455, and 1456, Prince Henry secured papal bulls from the Pope granting to himself and Portugal the exclusive right to explore the west coast of Africa. However, these bulls were ignored. For the most part, though, the early efforts of other Europeans were small individual ventures with no attempts made to establish permanent settlements in West Africa to rival those of Portugal.

COMPETITION FOR THE WEST AFRICAN SLAVE TRADE

While Portugal was busy exploring and colonizing West Africa, the Spanish were busy building their empire in the New World. By the middle of the sixteenth century Spain found herself in possession of Central and South American mines—the richest sources of precious metals then known to Europe—as well as of the Caribbean islands, which, while not rich in mineral wealth, were suited to the cultivation of crops that were in demand in Europe. In order to supplement the indigenous Indian labor force that was fast dying out under a brutal system of forced labor, Spain turned to West Africa. Since she did not possess settlements in West Africa, contracts were made in the 1530s with Portugal to supply slaves for the Spanish colonies in the New World, beginning the trans-Atlantic slave trade from West Africa to the West Indies and Central and South America.

The Dutch, after gaining their independence from Spain in 1572, set about to break the monopoly that Spain and Portugal had in the New World and West Africa. The Dutch succeeded in conquering major Portuguese possessions in the New World and immediately attempted to do the same in West Africa in order to benefit most from her New World conquest. By the middle of the seventeenth century, the Dutch had supplanted the Portuguese as the leading European power in West Africa and became the most active and best-organized agent in the trans-Atlantic slave trade, supplying Spanish, English, and Dutch settlers in the New World.

As the New World's demand for labor grew, the trans-Atlantic slave trade became highly competitive. The English, French, Swedes, Danes, Brandenburgers, and in time the Americans joined the Dutch and Portuguese in the business of buying and selling slaves. Eventually, however, in the eighteenth century, Great Britain emerged with a larger share of the external trade of West Africa than all other European nations combined.

In Africa itself, the French concentrated on the area around the mouth of the Senegal River. From Goree to Sherbro Island, the trade flourished, but no nation succeeded in securing a major share of it, even though Portugal claimed a great part of this coastline. Little attention was paid to the Grain and Ivory Coasts, because they lacked safe anchorages and landing places. The English, Dutch, Portuguese, Swedes, and Danes all maintained forts or slave factories along the Gold Coast, where the slave trade reached unparalleled heights. The slave trade along the Slave Coast and the Gulf of Guinea was conducted by individual merchants of all nations with no one nation dominating. Slaves were also brought from areas farther south along the west coast of Africa and some from as far as the island of Madagascar. But the majority of slaves who were transported to the New World came from West Africa.

THE CONDUCT OF THE SLAVE TRADE IN WEST AFRICA

In the very early days of the slave trade, West Africans living along the coast were kidnapped by European slave hunters. Because this practice antagonized the coastal rulers who had slaves they were willing to sell, a system of trade soon developed. When the demand for slaves began to exceed the exportable surplus, the coastal rulers began to seek other ways to secure more slaves. The practice of enslaving for crime and indebtedness became more common, and coastal kingdoms, with European stimulus, began to wage wars for the sole purpose of capturing slaves. Their economies firmly resting on the slave trade, the coastal forest states of Benin, Oyo, Dahomey, Akwamu, and Ashanti raided for slaves far into the interior of Africa.

Captured slaves were marched to the coast and housed in forts or slave factories, which had been constructed by the European traders, and here they awaited sale and shipment to the New World. The buying and selling of slaves on the coast of West Africa was a complicated business, because the spheres of influence of the indigenous rulers and Europeans differed from one area to another and because there was no common currency in use throughout West Africa or sometimes even within an individual kingdom. But once acceptable prices were agreed upon, the sale began. The slaves were closely inspected by the prospective purchaser. Those who were too young or too old, too sick or too infirm, were cast aside. Little regard was paid to family relationships: Wives were torn from their husbands and children from their parents. After the sale the selected slaves were branded with the mark of their purchaser and confined to ships anchored offshore or to the fort to await shipment.

Because the supply and demand varied from time to time and from place to place and because of the complicated system of trading, it is very difficult to give representative prices that were paid for slaves along the coast of Africa. But it was not uncommon to sell a slave in the New World for 50 to 100 percent more than what was paid in West Africa. Information that would indicate how many slaves actually reached the New World is also lacking. However, it is conservatively estimated that at least fifteen million reached the New World between the sixteenth and nineteenth centuries. There is no way of estimating the total number of those who lost their lives on account of the slave trade—those who were killed in the slave wars, those who were discarded and left to die along the coast because they were "unsalable," those who died during the Middle Passage, those who committed suicide rather than be enslaved, and those who were killed for inciting insurrections and revolts. It has been stated that for every slave reaching the New World, one died in West Africa or during the Middle Passage.

THE MIDDLE PASSAGE

The Middle Passage was the leg of the journey that brought the slaves from West Africa to the New World. Of all the horrible and inhumane experiences suffered by and inflicted on African blacks, this was by far the most cruel. After being taken aboard in chains, which were usually not removed until the slaver was two or three days at sea, slaves found themselves packed in the holds of ships having not as "much room as a man in his coffin" either in length or breadth. The men were separated from the women and children, but they were also wedged in like sardines in a can.

Conditions in such crowded quarters were frightful, especially during rough weather when the hatches were battened down or when tarpaulins were inadvertently thrown over the gratings. The heat was stifling, and many slaves found themselves chained to others who had died of suffocation. Sanitary conditions, if existing at all, were indescribable. Unable to prevent the necessities of nature from occurring, slaves relieved themselves as they lay shackled together in "spoon fashion." Oftentimes, stench emanating from a slaver could be smelled several miles downwind.

Disease was rife aboard ship. Smallpox was worst, but fevers and fluxes also caused many deaths. Measles, yellow fever, malaria, dysentery, and various viruses were fatal as well. Still others died from "fixed melancholy," or they committed suicide. "The Middle Passage was a crossroads and marketplace of diseases."

Fear dominated the minds of the crew. Not only was the crew exposed to the diseases and fevers aboard ship and to the revenge of the slaves who would mutiny given the slightest opportunity, but also there was the chance of the slaver being taken by pirates. Because of the danger of mutiny, rigid discipline was enforced; in spite of elaborate precautions mutinies were frequent and a few were even successful. Usually, however, insurrections meant diabolical retribution—whipping, dismemberment, beheading, walking-the-plank. When slavers ran short of food or water, proportionate numbers of slaves were "jettisoned," and after the slave trade was outlawed ship captains, fearing capture, sometimes cast their entire cargoes of slaves overboard. Cases of incurable disease and fever were similarly treated.

In good weather the slaves were allowed on deck. The men were attached by their leg irons to a chain that ran along the bulwarks of the ship, while the women and children were allowed to roam the deck. Under the watchful eye of a fearful crew, the slaves were given two meals a day, consisting of boiled rice, millet, or cornmeal with a few lumps of salt beef, or horsebeans boiled to pulp and mixed with palm oil, flour, water, and red pepper. Stewed yams and manioc or plantains were also a regular part of the diet. With the food, they were given a half-pint of water. In times other than good weather, the slaves were served in the hold where the heat was excessive and the floor was often covered with blood and waste. Those slaves who refused to eat were whipped or subjected to the "speculum oris"—an instrument used to forcibly open the mouth. As a therapeutic measure, the slaves were compelled to dance and sing. This was oftentimes done under the stimulus of a whip, for such a practice was torture for those in chains.

As stated before, there was a high fatality rate during the Middle Passage. A few voyages were made without the loss of a single slave, and in other voyages the entire shipload of slaves was lost. But these were the exceptional cases. Those records that are preserved indicate that the average loss was approximately 13 percent.

REFERENCES

Blake, John W., *European Beginnings in West Africa, 1454-1578* (New York: Longmans, Green and Co., 1937).

_____, ed, and trans., *Europeans in West Africa, 1450-1560* (London: Hakluyt Society, 1942).

Bosman, William, *A New and Accurate Description of the Coast of Guinea* (New York: Barnes & Noble, 1967).

Curtin, Phillip D., ed., *Africa Remembered: Narratives by West Africans from the Era of the Slave Trade* (Madison, Wis.: University of Wisconsin Press, 1967).

*Davidson, Basil, *The African Slave Trade: Precolonial History, 1450-1850* (Boston: Atlantic Monthly Press, 1961 [ALB, Little]).

Donnan, Elizabeth, *Documents Illustrative of the History of the Slave Trade to America* (Washington, D.C.: Carnegie Institute of Washington, 1930-1935).

Dowd, Jerome, "The African Slave Trade," *Journal of Negro History*, III (January 1917).

Du Bois, W. E. B., *Black Folk, Then and Now* (New York: Henry Holt and Co., 1939).

_____, *Suppression of the African Slave Trade to the United States of America, 1638-1870* (New York: Longmans, Green and Co., 1896).

Lloyd, Christopher, *The Navy and the Slave Trade* (New York: Longmans, Green and Co., 1949).

MacInnes, Charles M., *England and Slavery* (Bristol, England: Arrowsmith, 1934).

Major, R. H., *The Life of Prince Henry of Portugal, Surnamed the Navigator* (London: A. Asher & Co., 1868).

*Mannix, Daniel P., and Malcolm Cowley, *Black Cargoes: A History of the Atlantic Slave Trade, 1518-1865* (New York: Viking Press, 1962 [Viking Press]).

Owens, William A., *Slave Mutiny* (London: Peter Davies, 1953).

*Phillips, Ulrich B., *American Negro Slavery* (New York: D. Appleton & Co., 1918 [Louisiana State University Press, 1966]).

Weatherford, Willis D., *The Negro from Africa to America* (New York: George H. Doran Co., 1924).

*Williams, Eric, *Capitalism and Slavery* (Chapel Hill, N.C.: University of North Carolina Press, 1944 [G. P. Putnam's Sons]).

Wyndham, Hugh A., *The Atlantic and Slavery* (New York: Oxford University Press, 1935).

3
Plantation Life in the West Indies

ARRIVAL IN THE WEST INDIES

Although slaves were used in mining on the mainland of Central and South America, it was in the West Indies that slavery began its really significant growth in the New World. The islands produced a variety of commodities including indigo, coffee, cotton, tobacco, hides, and ginger, but it was sugar more than any other product that created the great demand for slaves.

Upon arrival in the West Indies, slaves were taken directly to the plantation if the owner's agent had purchased them in West Africa. However, if they were purchased by a middleman in West Africa, the slaves were required to go through the same type of sale that they had experienced in West Africa. At times an entire shipload of slaves was bought by a slave merchant, who herded them from island to island, selling a few here and a few there, until all had been sold. In the course of the sale, the few families that had survived the vicissitudes through which they had gone from the time of their capture to their arrival in the islands were almost certain to be dispersed.

Once on the plantation, new slaves had to go through a "seasoning" period, that is, the time necessary to accustom them to their new environment. This period lasted from one to three years, after which they became an integral part of the everyday plantation labor force.

LIFE ON A WEST INDIAN PLANTATION

Life on West Indian plantations varied from place to place and from time to time, but by and large it was very dangerous and brutalizing. Because the owners of plantations generally did not live on the island but in Europe, the institutions that would have had some ameliorating effect on the treatment of the slaves were never fully established. Plantations were generally left in the hands of overseers whose primary motive was to make as much profit as possible, and their treatment of the slaves was unlikely to be scrutinized provided they raised a good crop.

The average work day lasted from ten to twelve hours with two brief periods for meals and rest. During the harvest the work day was extended from fourteen to eighteen hours, and the rest periods were sometimes abandoned. Men, women, and children worked in the fields and in the mills under the stimulus of a whip and gun.

Food was inadequate. Slaves received weekly rations of meal and salt pork, which was sometimes supplemented by fish, beans, and syrup. Many of the foodstuffs were imported to the islands because of the owners' insatiable desire to grow only cash crops. Additional food was sometimes secured by slaves who hunted, fished, or gardened on Sundays and holidays. Clothing was scanty. Once a year slaves were given clothing, which generally consisted of overalls and shirts for the men and calico shifts for the women. Children often went naked until they reached the age of four or five, at which time they were given shifts to wear.

Slave houses were small and ill constructed. There were no furnishings save those that the slaves could construct or pieces that they could salvage. Bedding consisted of naked boards or of mattresses made of a material such as corn shucks. Under such conditions, regular family life was often impossible. Slave mortality was notoriously high. The average work life of a full field hand was seven to twelve years. Many planters considered it cheaper to buy slaves than to breed them, and therefore many slaves were literally worked to death. The house slaves and skilled artisans (most of whom were mulattoes) and town slaves were better fed and better clothed and worked fewer hours than the plantation field hands, but they too were subject to harsh punishment by "the jumper," a professional whipper.

THE WEST INDIAN SLAVE CODES

Each colony in the West Indies had a body of laws that regulated the conduct of the slaves, though these codes varied from colony to colony. Especially in the English islands, slaves were considered to be chattel property, having no social, civil, political, or economic rights. The codes in the Spanish, Portuguese and, to some extent, French colonies were less drastic than those in the English. They bore down less harshly on the slaves with respect to marriage, civil rights, education, and manumission. Application of the codes also varied considerably. During quiet times the codes were not always rigorously enforced, but during a revolt or even when there was a rumor of one, the codes were strictly adhered to.

SLAVE REVOLTS IN THE WEST INDIES

If cruel treatment was designed to prevent uprisings, running away, or resistance to other acts, it was unsuccessful. Throughout the history of the institution of slavery in the West Indies, there were revolts and other manifestations of discontent. Runaways proved so troublesome on some islands that the colonial government entered into peace treaties with groups of these "maroons" who had settled in the mountains.

One of the most serious insurrections took place in Santo Domingo in 1758 under the leadership of Macandal. Elaborate plans were made to drive the whites off the island, but the plot was discovered and suppressed. Finally in 1791, slaves under the leadership of Toussaint L'Ouverture successfully revolted, and the French colony of Santo Domingo soon thereafter became Haiti, an independent black republic—the first in the New World.

DECLINE OF SLAVERY IN THE WEST INDIES

By the turn of the nineteenth century, West Indian slavery was becoming increasingly less profitable. Indeed, the typical West Indian plantation was operating at a loss. The world market was glutted with sugar, and soil exhaustion was beginning to take its toll. As a result, there was a drastic decline in the demand for slaves in the islands, though later it picked up in the Spanish colony of Cuba.

REFERENCES

Aimes, Hubert H. S., *A History of Slavery in Cuba, 1511 to 1868* (New York: G. P. Putnam's Sons, 1907).

*Andrews, Charles M., *The Colonial Period of American History* (New Haven, Conn.: Yale University Press, 1934-1938 [Yale University Press]).

Burns, Sir Alan, *History of the British West Indies* (London: Allen & Unwin, 1954).

Curtin, Philip, *Two Jamaicas: The Role of Ideas in a Tropical Colony, 1630-1865* (Cambridge, Mass: Harvard University Press, 1955).

Edwards, Bryan, *A History, Civil and Commercial, of the British Colonies in the West Indies*, 3 vols. (London: Printed for J. Stockdale, Vol. 2, 1794).

Goveia, Elsa, *Slave Society in the British Leeward Islands at the End of the Eighteenth Century* (New Haven, Conn.: Yale University Press, 1965).

*James, C. L. R., *The Black Jacobins: Toussaint L'Ouverture and the Santo Domingo Revolution* (London: Seeker & Warbing, 1938 [Vintage]).

Newton, A. P., *The European Nations in the West Indies, 1493-1688* (London: A. & C. Black, Ltd., 1933).

*Phillips, Ulrich B., *American Negro Slavery* (New York: D. Appleton & Co., 1918 [Louisiana State University Press]).

Pitman, F. W., *The Development of the British West Indies, 1700-1763* (New Haven, Conn.: Yale University Press, 1917).

Ragatz, Lowell J., *The Fall of the Planter Class in the British Caribbean* (New York: The Century Co., 1928).

Renny, Robert, *A History of Jamaica* (London: J. Cawthorn, 1807).

4
America: Black Explorers and the Evolution of Slavery

BLACKS IN AMERICA DURING PRE-COLONIAL TIMES

The purchase of twenty blacks in 1619 by the colonial government at Jamestown, Virginia, was not the first contact of blacks with the Western Hemisphere. According to some authorities, long before Europeans established a claim to lands in the Western Hemisphere, black Africans had visited its shores and penetrated far into the interior.

More important is the fact that blacks had a place among the exploits of the European pioneers who many years later explored North and South America. Pedro Alonso Nino, a pilot in Columbus' fleet, has been referred to as a black. In the discovery of the Pacific Ocean, Balboa's party included thirty blacks. In the conquest of Mexico, Cortez was aided by many blacks, one of whom planted some grains of wheat and thus made himself a pioneer in wheat raising in the New World. Blacks assisted in the exploration of Guatemala and the conquests of Chile, Peru, and Venezuela. Blacks were with Lucas Vasquez de Ayllon in his expedition from Florida northward and figured prominently in the establishment of the settlement of San Miguel at the mouth of the Pee Dee River in South Carolina. They accompanied Narvaez and his successor, Cabeza de Vaca, through what is now the southwestern part of the United States. They were with Alarcon and

Coronado in the conquest of what is now New Mexico, and they were ordered imported by De Soto, the explorer of the lower Mississippi Valley. Blacks were also with the early French explorers. Although there is not concrete evidence that they were with Cartier and Champlain, it is certain that they did accompany the Jesuits in Canada and the Mississippi Valley during the seventeenth century. They also constituted a considerable element in the exploration and settlement of Louisiana.

The majority of blacks who accompanied the Spanish, Portuguese, and French explorers were slaves who served as laborers and domestic servants. But there were also a few free blacks, including some skilled artisans. The most celebrated black man during pre-colonial times was Estevanico, or "Little Stephen," a member of the Narvaez expedition. He preceded the main force, reporting observations he made and sending back directions for the expedition. He was the first non-Native American to cross what is now New Mexico, Arizona, and northern Mexico.

EVOLUTION OF THE INSTITUTION OF SLAVERY

In August 1619, the colonial government at Jamestown, Virginia, purchased twenty blacks from a Dutch frigate and thus commenced the importation of black people into North America for the purpose of servile labor that was to last for some 250 years. During the first forty years some Afro-Americans were accorded the status of indentured servants—a status given to whites who had bound themselves for a number of years to work for those who had paid for their passage to the New World. Some of these Afro-Americans served out their terms of indenture, became free citizens, acquired property, and became the owners of indentured servants and slaves. From 1640, however, there is evidence that some Afro-Americans in Maryland and Virginia were being held as slaves.

As the demands for labor increased and as the colonists found that the use of white indentured servants and Indians for servile labor was unsatisfactory, they began to look to the blacks, the supply of whom seemed inexhaustible, whose temperament was said to be suited for chattel slavery, and whose physical characteristics made them easily distinguishable in the community. Consequently, each of the colonies began to give recognition to the institution of slavery. By custom, court decision, or legislation, the Afro-American's status was reduced to that of a slave. In some, and perhaps all, of the English colonies the idea that blacks would be enslaved was reinforced by the example set by the Spanish and Portuguese—from whom the English borrowed the term "Negro," which meant "black." From its inception slavery was an economic success in the southern colonies. With its mild climate and fertile soil, the South reaped many benefits by using slaves to cultivate the crops that were then in demand. Hence, the vast majority of slaves were used on plantations in the cultivation of the great staples—rice, indigo, and tobacco. Other slaves worked as domestics or as unskilled laborers in nonagricultural pursuits. Because of the acute shortage of white artisans and mechanics, many slaves were also trained in the skilled trades.

As an economic institution slavery never became deeply entrenched in the middle colonies and New England. The predominantly commercial and mixed-farming economy in this area did not encourage the large-scale employment of slave labor. In certain areas such as Rhode Island and the counties around New York, however, there were appreciable numbers of blacks. For the most part they worked as farm hands, domestics, or unskilled or skilled laborers in the urban centers. Because of the thin soil, the harsh climate, and the relatively commercial nature of the area slavery never developed into an important economic institution in the northern colonies. But even though slaves were not used in large numbers, it should be remembered that many northern shippers and merchants gained the benefits of the slave trade and its allied industries during the first half of the eighteenth century. In Rhode Island, especially, enslavement of Africans throughout the British colonies helped support a major domestic industry, the distilling of rum.

REFERENCES

Ballagh, James C., *A History of Slavery in Virginia* (Baltimore, Md.: Johns Hopkins Press, 1902).

Bassett, John S., *Slavery and Servitude in the Colony of North Carolina* (Baltimore, Md.: Johns Hopkins Press, 1896).

Bolton, H. E., and T. M. Marshall, *The Colonization of North America, 1492–1783* (New York: The Macmillan Co., 1920).

Bracket, J. R., *The Negro in Maryland: A Study of the Institution of Slavery* (Baltimore, Md.: Johns Hopkins Press, 1899).

Browning, James B., *Negro Companions of the Spanish Pioneers in the New World* (Washington, D. C.: Howard University Studies in History, 1931).

Bruce, Phillip A., *Economic History of Virginia in the Seventeenth Century: An Inquiry Into the Material Condition of the People, Based on Original and Contemporaneous Books* (New York: The Macmillan Co., 1896).

Cooley, H. S., *A Study of Slavery in New Jersey* (Baltimore, Md.: Johns Hopkins Press, 1896).

Davis, T. R., "Negro Servitude in the United States," *Journal of Negro History*, VIII (July 1923).

Flanders, R., *Plantation Slavery in Georgia* (Chapel Hill, N.C.: University of North Carolina Press, 1933).

*Greene, L. J., *The Negro in Colonial New England* (New York: Kennikat Press, 1942 [Atheneum]).

Harrissee, Henry, *The Discovery of North America* (London: H. Stevens & Son, 1892).

Klingberg, F. J., *An Appraisal of the Negro in South Carolina: A Study in Americanization* (Washington, D.C.: Associated Publishers, Inc., 1941).

Logan, Rayford W., "Estevanico, Negro Discoverer of the Southwest," *Phylon*, I (4th Quarter, 1940).

Lowery, Woodbury, *The Spanish Settlements Within the Present Limits of the United States, 1513-1561* (New York: Russell & Russell, 1959).

McKee, S., *Labor in Colonial New York, 1664-1776* (London: P. S. King & Son, Ltd., 1935).

McManus, Edgar J., *A History of Negro Slavery in New York* (Syracuse, N. Y.: Syracuse University Press, 1966).

*Moore, G. H., *Notes on the History of Slavery in Massachusetts* (New York: D. Appleton & Co., 1866 [New York: Negro University Press, 1968]).

Rippy, J. F., "The Negro and Spanish Pioneers in the New World," *Journal of Negro History*, VI (April 1921).

Russell, John H., *The Free Negro in Virginia, 1619-1865* (Baltimore, Md.: Johns Hopkins Press, 1913).

Steiner, Bernard C., *History of Slavery in Connecticut* (Baltimore, Md.: Johns Hopkins University Press, 1893).

Turner, E. R., *The Negro in Pennsylvania, Slavery-Servitude-Freedom, 1639-1861* (Washington, D. C.: The American Historical Association, 1911).

Wax, Darold D., "Quaker Merchants and the Slave Trade in Colonial Pennsylvania," *Pennsylvania Magazine of History and Biography*, LXXXVI (April 1962).

Winsor, Justin, ed., *Narrative and Critical History of America* (New York: Houghton Mifflin Co., 1884-1889).

Wright, Richard R., "Negro Companions of the Spanish Explorers," *Phylon*, II (4th Quarter, 1941).

5
Slave Resistance and Colonial Controls

SLAVE RESISTANCE IN COLONIAL TIMES

Historians who have pictured slavery as a beneficent or necessary institution have had little or no place in their works for accounts of the efforts by slaves to avoid or challenge the system. Because the institution was inherently brutal, the basic attitude of slaves was very often one of recalcitrance and sometimes of active defiance. The record is replete with evidence indicating that from the earliest times blacks fought courageously against being enslaved. In the slave wars in Africa, they fiercely resisted. On the slave ships they mutinied whenever the opportunity presented itself. And they carried their struggle for freedom to the colonies in North America— into a society that did everything it could to suppress them.

The resistance of slaves took many forms. Many ran away, idled at their tasks, feigned illness, and damaged or stole property. Some burned crops, barns, and houses; others killed whites, usually their owners or overseers; and some even maimed or killed themselves in desperation.

The form of resistance that whites dreaded most was the revolt. Generally, revolts were small and ill organized, but there were several that were fairly extensive and well planned. Regardless of size, however, most were discovered prior to fruition and quelled with tyrannical ferocity. More slaves than whites died in these struggles for liberty.

COLONIAL SLAVE CODES

With the legalization of slavery and the increased slave population, the colonies began to adopt slave codes. The codes, sometimes an outgrowth of the laws governing indentured servants and sometimes patterned after the West Indian slave codes, were negative in character and were aimed at repressing slave insurrections as well as controlling slave conduct. In the southern colonies they were very elaborate and generally deprived the slaves of virtually all civil, judicial, economic, social, political, familial, and intellectual rights.

Some features common to the more complete codes were:

a. Slaves were declared to be chattel property, which could be bought and sold at the will of the owner.

b. The avenues of manumission were greatly restricted.

c. All business dealings of slaves had to be done through their white masters.

d. Slaves could not bear firearms.

e. Slaves could not buy or consume alcoholic beverages.

f. Slaves could not vote.

g. The right of assembly was restricted.

h. The right of free speech was nonexistent.

i. The right to travel was restricted.

j. The right to a fair and impartial trial was nonexistent.

k. The right to obtain an education was nonexistent.

The types of punishment meted out to a slave for violation of the codes depended on the nature of the crime, the colony in which the crime took place, and the time when the act was committed. Except for capital crimes, during peaceful times there was a tendency to work slaves hard and to pay little attention to the law. But during and after an actual or rumored insurrection the codes were usually rigorously enforced.

The slave codes of the southern colonies, especially of South Carolina and Georgia, were enforced with brutal discipline. Capital crimes were numerous, and burning, branding, maiming, cropping, and whipping were the usual means of punishment. In comparison to the codes of the southern colonies, the codes of the northern colonies were not extensive, especially in Pennsylvania where the Quaker influence was predominant. There were fewer capital crimes and the customary means of punishment was the whip.

Some colonies had laws that restricted the conduct of the masters with reference to the treatment of their slaves. But if a master were brought to trial for mistreating a slave, very rarely would he be convicted, because no slaves could testify against white men; even if he were convicted, the punishment was usually a small fine.

REFERENCES

*Aptheker, Herbert, *American Negro Slave Revolts* (New York: International Publishers, 1963 [International Publishers]).

Clarke, T. Wood, "The Negro Plot of 1741," *New York History*, XXV (April 1944).

*Cobb, Thomas R. R., *An Inquiry Into the Law of Negro Slavery in the United States of America* (Philadelphia: T. & J. W. Johnson & Co., 1858 [Savannah: W. T. Williams]).

Goodell, William, "The American Slave Code in Theory and Practice," *American and Foreign Antislavery Society*, IX (1853).

*Herskovits, Melville J., *Myth of the Negro Past* (New York: Harper & Brothers, 1941 [Boston: Beacon Press, 1958]).

*Hurd, John C., *The Law of Freedom and Bondage in the United States* (Boston: Little, Brown and Co., 1858 [New York: Negro University Press, 1968]).

*Jordan, Winthrop D., *White Over Black: American Attitudes Toward the Negro, 1550-1812* (Chapel Hill, N.C.: University of North Carolina Press, 1968 [Penguin, 1969]).

Scott, Kenneth, "The Slave Insurrection in New York in 1712," *New York Historical Society Quarterly*, XLV (January 1961).

Stroud, George M., *A Sketch of the Laws Relating to Slavery in the Several States of the United States of America* (Philadelphia: Kimber & Sharpless, 1827).

6
Religion and Antislavery Sentiment

RELIGION AND SLAVERY

Little is known about the survival of African religious beliefs in the colonies. It is safe to say, however, that the slave trade and working conditions in North America combined to deprive Afro-Americans of opportunity to practice these beliefs. Some were offered an alternative—Christianity.

The New England Puritans believed that everyone, including Afro-Americans, should be given religious training, though they sometimes failed to provide it in practice. Quakers were reluctant to admit blacks into their sect, but they did encourage blacks to join other churches. In the South, the established Anglican Church made some not very effective efforts to Christianize slaves through its London-based missionary branch, the Society for the Propagation of the Gospel in Foreign Parts. Because the missionaries had to gain the consent of slaveholders in order to preach to slaves, they stressed that Christianity would make slaves more docile and more diligent in their work. In their sermons to slaves they emphasized the duty of slaves to be faithful and obedient. For many reasons, including the sheer number of slaves, these efforts met with only scattered success.

Much more effective were two evangelical denominations that emerged in America in the second half of the eighteenth century, the Baptist and Methodist Churches. The revivalistic fervor of Baptist and Methodist preachers seems to have been welcomed by increasing numbers of Afro-

Americans. Some all-black churches were organized, as well as many integrated ones. By 1800 many Afro-Americans, particularly in Virginia, had joined these churches. An equally significant development was the appearance of black ministers, mostly Baptist, who preached on plantations and in black, integrated, and even all-white churches.

COLONIAL ANTISLAVERY SENTIMENT

Almost as soon as slavery had become fully rooted in America, a few slaves, free Afro-Americans, and white abolitionists protested publicly against slavery as well as against the slave trade. While some whites protested against the slave trade, frequently they were not opposed to slavery in principle. Among these were skilled white artisans who felt that slave labor posed an economic threat to their livelihood. Others expressed the fear that revolts would result from the unrestricted importation of slaves.

Although slavery was attacked by one prominent New England Puritan, most simply accepted the institution until the eve of the Revolution. It was the Quakers, located mainly in the middle colonies and especially in Pennsylvania, who believed most firmly in social as well as spiritual equality. From the very outset, a few agitated for the abolition of the slave trade and the emancipation of the slaves. After 1750 the Quakers gradually moved as a body and finally decided that members who retained the ownership of slaves after a designated time would be excommunicated. Consequently, by the time of the Revolutionary War, through the use of moral persuasion or religious coercion, most Quakers had liberated their slaves.

During the dozen years of agitation that culminated in America's war for independence, many colonists saw the inconsistency between their cries for liberty and equality and their maintenance of a system of chattel slavery. The result was widespread demands for abolition of slavery, demands which came from every state except South Carolina and Georgia. Many Afro-Americans, free and slave, understood the inconsistency between the revolutionary philosophies and the institution of slavery, too, and in the North, at least, they published their case for liberty in terms of liberty for all.

REFERENCES

*Beard, Charles A., *An Economic Interpretation of the Constitution* (New York: The Macmillan Co., 1935 [Free Press]).

Drake, T. E., *Quakers and Slavery in America* (New Haven, Conn.: Yale University Press, 1950).

Du Bois, W. E. B., ed., *The Negro Church* (Atlanta: Atlanta University Press, 1903).

*Farrand, Max, ed., *Records of the Federal Convention of 1787* (New Haven, Conn.: Yale University Press, 1911 [Yale University Press]).

James, Sydney V., *A People Among Peoples: Quaker Benevolence in Eighteenth Century America* (Cambridge, Mass.: Harvard University Press, 1963).

*Jameson, J. F., *The American Revolution Considered as a Social Movement* (Boston: Beacon Press, 1960 [Princeton University Press]).

Jones, R. M., *The Quakers in the American Colonies* (New York: The Macmillan Co., 1911).

*Jordan, Winthrop D., *White Over Black: American Attitudes Toward the Negro, 1550–1812* (Chapel Hill, N.C.: University of North Carolina Press, 1968 [Penguin, 1969]).

Locke, Mary S., *Antislavery in America from the Introduction of African Slaves to the Prohibition of the Slave Trade (1619–1808)* (Boston: Ginn & Co., 1901).

Woodson, Carter G., *The History of the Negro Church* (Washington, D. C.: Associated Publishers, Inc., 1921).

7
The Afro-American and the Revolutionary War

THE REVOLUTIONARY WAR

It is estimated that there were 300,000 colonial troops in the Revolutionary War. Approximately 5000 of these were Afro-Americans, with the vast majority coming from the northern urban centers. During colonial times, the general policy in most of the colonies had been to exclude Afro-Americans from the militia. But when there were manpower shortages most of the colonies took a calculated risk and armed Afro-Americans, especially during times of war. Hence, during the French and Indian wars and in Indian skirmishes, Afro-Americans served in most colonial militias.

Afro-Americans served in the colonial militias during the early months of the Revolutionary War, taking part in all of the initial military engagements—the Battles of Concord, Lexington, and Bunker Hill. Shortly thereafter, however, the Continental Congress adopted a resolution recommending that all Afro-Americans be discharged from the Continental Army. Because of agitation by the colonists and Afro-Americans themselves and the soliciting of Afro-Americans by the British, this policy was soon modified to allow the reenlistment of those Afro-Americans who were then serving in the Continental Army but no others.

In time, due to the critical manpower shortage, it became necessary to further relax the policy of nonutilization of Afro-Americans in the Continental Army, and Afro-Americans, free and slave, were allowed to enlist in the Continental Army as well as in the individual colonial militias. The institution of the quota and substitution systems also facilitated the enlistment of blacks. The policy was liberalized to such an extent that by the end of the war, blacks, free and slave, were allowed to enlist in all colonial militias except those of Georgia and South Carolina. In the Continental Army Afro-Americans were integrated into white fighting units, but generally they were assigned to functions in support of military operations or detailed to some menial task. Afro-American drummers and fifers were also common. Only a small number of blacks were armed and actually fought.

From the beginning of the Revolutionary War Afro-Americans were able to enlist in the Continental Navy and the navies of the individual colonies. They were also welcomed aboard commissioned privateers. In the Navy, the majority served as officer's boys, mess boys, or powder boys. A few, especially on board privateers, were assigned to more meaningful tasks such as pilots. Although not formally inducted into the Continental forces, Afro-Americans also served as spies, scouts, guides, messengers, and military laborers. Even in the South where recruitment of Afro-Americans was forbidden, slaves were impressed into service or were purchased or hired by Army officials to perform servile labor.

Because the British suffered manpower shortages from the outset of the war, they were always receptive to utilizing Afro-Americans. British officials issued proclamations offering freedom to slaves who ran away and served with the British forces. Counterproclamations were issued by the colonists and other devices were employed in order to prevent the slaves from running over to the British, but thousands of Afro-Americans—free and slave—defected. The British made use of the Afro-Americans in much the same manner that the colonists did. They, too, were reluctant to arm Afro-Americans. When the war came to an end, the British, in spite of protest by the colonists, sailed away with over fifteen thousand Afro-Americans, the majority of whom were reenslaved in other British colonies. The same fate awaited some Afro-Americans who served in the Continental forces under the provision that they would be free after their term of service, though others actually earned their freedom by fighting for the patriot cause.

POST-REVOLUTIONARY WAR REACTION

After the Revolutionary War the impetus given to uplift the Afro-American was gradually checked. And yet, some forces had been set in motion before and during the war that brought about a change. Numerous persons of stature spoke out against the institution of slavery, and anti slavery societies became more widespread. Legislation against the African slave trade, which was initially passed to combat England, continued after the war. Indeed, South Carolina was the only state to reopen the African slave trade after once banning it. Northern and some middle states, by legislation, court decision, or constitutional provision, gradually outlawed slavery by providing that Afro-Americans born after a certain date were to be free.

Despite the efforts of antislavery leaders, they were unable to abolish the slave trade universally or to emancipate the slaves. South of Pennsylvania, to be sure, there had been considerable antislavery sentiment expressed by the representatives to the Continental Congress, but the delegates to the Constitutional Convention of 1787 did not wish to concern themselves with the Afro-American problem. They were primarily concerned with the formation of a national government. The question of the Afro-American belonged to the individual states.

The position of the delegates regarding the Afro-American changed when the matters of taxes, representation, fugitive slaves, and the slave trade were discussed. Northern merchants, already allied with southern planters in the slave trade and other commercial activities, lent their indirect endorsement to slavery. The result was the drafting of a constitution that, while avoiding the use of the words *slave* or *slavery*, promoted the institution of slavery in three places: (1) Article I, Section 2: For purposes of representation and direct taxes, slaves should be counted as three-fifths of a person; (2) Article I, Section 9: The federal government could not interfere with the slave trade until 1808; and (3) Article IV, Section 2: Fugitive slaves had to be returned to their masters.

After the ratification of the U.S. Constitution, the federal government adopted a hands-off policy with reference to the Afro-American. Like the delegates at the Constitutional Convention, the federal government believed that the Afro-American problem was a state problem. Only two laws directly affecting Afro-Americans were passed by the federal government: the Fugitive Slave Act of 1793 and the law banning the African slave trade as of January 1, 1808.

REFERENCES

Du Bois, W. E. B., *Suppression of the African Slave Trade to the United States of America, 1638-1870* (New York: Russell & Russell, 1965).

*Farrand, Max, ed., *The Records of the Federal Convention of 1787* (New Haven: Yale University Press, 1911 [Yale University Press]).

Hartgrove, W. B., "The Negro Soldier in the American Revolution," *Journal of Negro History*, I (April 1916).

*Jordan, Winthrop, *White Over Black: American Attitudes Toward the Negro, 1550-1812* (Chapel Hill, N.C.: University of North Carolina Press, 1968 [Penguin, 1969]).

Livermore, G., *An Historical Research Respecting the Opinions of the Founders of the Republic on Negroes as Slaves, as Citizens, and as Soldiers* (Boston: J. Wilson & Son, 1862).

Lynd, Staughton, "On Turner, Beard and Slavery," *Journal of Negro History*, XLVIII (October 1963).

Mazyek, Walter H., *George Washington and the Negro* (Washington, D. C.: Associated Publishers, Inc., 1932).

Moore, George H., *Historical Notes on the Employment of Negroes in the American Army of the American Revolution* (New York: C. T. Evans, 1862).

Nell, William C., *The Colored Patriots of the American Revolution* (New York: Arno and *The New York Times*, 1968).

*Quarles, Benjamin, *The Negro in the American Revolution* (Chapel Hill, N.C.: University of North Carolina Press, 1967).

*Van Doren, Carl, *The Great Rehearsal: The Story of the Making and Ratifying of the Constitution of the United States* (New York: Viking Press, 1948 [Viking]).

Zilversmit, Arthur, *The First Emancipation: The Abolition of Slavery in the North* (Chicago: The University of Chicago Press, 1967).

8
"Free" Afro-Americans

THE UNWANTED FREEDMAN

At the turn of the nineteenth century there were approximately sixty thousand free Afro-Americans, constituting 7.9 percent of the total Afro-American population. The majority of the free Afro-Americans lived in the urban centers of the North and in Maryland and Delaware.

This segment of the Afro-American population came about as a result of Afro-American indentured servants who completed their terms of indenture; slaves who were freed after serving in the armed forces; slaves who were freed as a result of the passage of legislation providing for emancipation; and slaves who were freed by private acts of manumission, by deed of gift, by self-purchase, by will, or by flight.

In the South

Free Afro-Americans were totally unwanted. They were thought to have criminal inclinations, to be improvident, and likely to become public charges. The chief objection to their presence was that it endangered the institution of slavery. Free Afro-Americans were said to be guilty of an entire catalogue of sins, including receiving stolen goods from slaves, selling slaves liquor, harboring runaway slaves, and inciting slave revolts.

Increasingly, by law and court decision, attempts were made to control the conduct of free Afro-Americans. From state to state, county to county, and city to city, the extensiveness of the controls and their application varied, depending primarily on the number of free Afro-Americans and the temper of the times, but some controls common throughout the South were:

1. Free Afro-Americans had the burden of proving that they were not slaves. This they did by carrying a certificate of freedom. Uncertified Afro-Americans were treated as runaway slaves, subject to being jailed, hired out, or sold at public auction. In some states free Afro-Americans had to have white guardians to whom they reported periodically.
2. Free Afro-Americans could be reduced to servitude if they failed to pay their debts, taxes, fines, or court fees.
3. Free Afro-Americans could not hold public office, and in most states could not vote.
4. Generally, free Afro-Americans could not testify against a white person nor were they permitted to possess or purchase firearms without special permission.
5. Free Afro-Americans could not purchase liquor without a recommendation from a "reputable" white person.
6. Free Afro-Americans had to observe curfew laws and were generally denied the right of assembly.
7. Free Afro-Americans were often segregated in places of public accommodation and educational institutions.

Even in the face of the many restrictions, however, there were opportunities for free Afro-Americans in the South to make a living. Because of the acute shortage of white skilled laborers, the free Afro-American had the opportunity to work in the trades. A few were able to accumulate substantial amounts of property, and some even became the owners of slaves.

In the North
Because the doctrine of white supremacy was held as tenaciously in the North as in the South, the status of free Afro-Americans in the North was not unlike that of their southern counterparts. Nevertheless, they encountered fewer restrictions, they could sometimes protest against them, and they had somewhat greater opportunities for self-expression. As in the South, laws and court decisions governed their conduct. In many states free Afro-Americans could not vote, they could not testify against whites, they were barred from jury service, places of public accommodation were closed to them, and they had to attend segregated schools or none at all.

In making a living free Afro-Americans faced more difficulties in the North than in the South. Their fields of employment were generally confined to common labor and domestic service, and after 1830, even these menial jobs were increasingly unavailable, since they were being taken by the almost five million white immigrants who arrived between 1830 and 1860. Furthermore, trade unions were closed to them. Despite the many laws, court decisions, and the established custom, a few free Afro-Americans became "well-to-do." Most northern cities had their Afro-American food caterers, barbers, tailors, and small businessmen. There were also a few Afro-American fur traders and farmers.

As the number of free Afro-Americans increased, many felt that they must be sent out of the country. In the South, slave owners believed that complete discipline of the slaves was impossible as long as free Afro-Americans remained. In the North it was felt that the two races could never live together in peace and harmony. Consequently, the possibility of colonizing the Afro-American arose. Serious proposals were first frequently advanced after the Revolutionary War, especially in Virginia. The great majority of Afro-Americans and northern abolitionists were adamantly opposed to colonization and especially to the American Colonization Society, which was founded in 1816. With the aid of the federal and state governments, the Society established the colony of Liberia in 1821 for Afro-Americans who wished to leave the United States. The efforts of the Society to deport Afro-Americans were unrewarding, for it is estimated that less than fifteen thousand Afro-Americans were relocated outside the United States.

BLACK SELF-IMPROVEMENT

In the early 1800s, the atmosphere in which Afro-Americans lived, whether North or South, was oppressive. In the South, the institution of slavery was becoming more entrenched, and the status of many free Afro-Americans was not much better than that of the slave. In the North, where laws were fast putting an end to the institution of slavery, Afro-Americans still could not express much optimism or any great faith in the future. In this atmosphere ladened with subservience and subordination, Afro-Americans had to seek ways of bettering their lot, independent of the whites.

Some of the first Afro-Americans to achieve some measure of intellectual freedom and economic self-sufficiency were Jupiter Hammon (writer), Gustavus Vassa (writer), Phyllis Wheatley (poet), Benjamin

Banneker (mathematician, astronomer, and surveyor), and Paul Cuffee (shipowner). These and others were pointed to as examples in refuting the growing charges that Afro-Americans were inherently inferior to whites. In the effort to improve their status in the post-Revolutionary War period, Afro-Americans found it necessary to establish separate institutions. Independent churches sprang up, and in a number of northern cities, organizations of a benevolent and fraternal nature were established. Afro-Americans took advantage of and benefited from the general trend to establish and improve schools, though frequently they were excluded. Afro-Americans founded literary societies, libraries, and reading rooms in their struggle for self-improvement.

After 1830 Afro-Americans throughout the nation began to meet and collectively protest against their status. This movement, called the Negro Convention Movement, gave free Afro-Americans the opportunity to petition collectively the state and federal governments and otherwise apprise the nation of the Afro-American's stand on public issues. But after the national conventions had adjourned, the delegates dispersed, doing very little in their communities to carry out plans they had adopted. Furthermore, some Afro-Americans refused to participate in the Movement because they felt that an organization made up exclusively of Afro-Americans tacitly accepted segregation.

REFERENCES

Andrews, C. C., *History of the New York African Free Schools* (New York: M. Day, 1830).

Brawley, Benjamin, *Early Negro American Writers* (Chapel Hill, N.C.: University of North Carolina Press, 1935).

Fox, E. L., *The American Colonization Society, 1817–1840* (Baltimore, Md.: Johns Hopkins University Press, 1919).

Franklin, John H., *The Free Negro in North Carolina, 1790–1860* (Chapel Hill, N.C.: University of North Carolina Press, 1943).

Hogan, W. R., and Edwin A. Davis, eds., *William Johnson's Natchez: The Antebellum Diary of a Free Negro* (Baton Rouge, La.: Louisiana State University Press, 1951).

*Litwack, Leon F., *North of Slavery: The Negro in the Free States, 1790–1860* (Chicago: The University of Chicago Press, 1961 [Phoenix, The University of Chicago Press]).

Mehlinger, Louis R., "The Attitude of the Free Negro Toward African Colonization," *Journal of Negro History*, I (July 1916).

Russell, John H., *The Free Negro in Virginia, 1619–1865* (Baltimore, Md.: Johns Hopkins University Press, 1913).

Sherwood, Henry N., "Paul Cuffee," *Journal of Negro History*, VIII (April 1923).

Staudenraus, P. J., *The American Colonization Movement, 1816–1865* (New York: Columbia University Press, 1961).

Wesley, Charles H., *Richard Allen, Apostle of Freedom* (Washington, D.C.: Associated Publishers, Inc., 1935).

Woodson, Carter G., *Education of the Negro Prior to 1861* (New York: G. P. Putnam's Sons, 1915).

_____, *Free Negro Heads of Families in the United States in 1830* (Washington, D.C.: Association for the Study of Negro Life and History, 1925).

_____, *History of the Negro Church* (Washington, D.C.: Associated Publishers, 1921).

9
The Afro-American and the War of 1812

The principal reason for the War of 1812 was the impressment of American seamen, Afro-American and white, by the British. War was declared on June 18, 1812, and Congress called for fifty thousand volunteers. Conscription was proposed in 1814 but never adopted.

From the outset of the war, free Afro-Americans enlisted in the United States Navy, where the policy was one of total acceptance. The exact number of Afro-Americans who served in the Navy is not known because reference to race was often omitted from ships' rosters. But judging from what records we do have, it can be assumed that there was scarcely an American war vessel whose crew did not include Afro-Americans. Like the Afro-American sailors during the Revolutionary War, they served in the mess, but they could also be found in some instances at the gun, on the yardarm, and in the gangway.

Afro-Americans offered their services in the United States Army when the call went out for volunteers, but their efforts to enlist, even in separate organizations, were futile. New York was the only state to specifically authorize the recruitment of black soldiers. After many battles had been lost and white enlistments slackened, utilization of the Afro-American as a soldier was seriously considered, especially when the British were preparing to invade Louisiana. Realizing that he lacked the manpower necessary to defend the area, General Andrew Jackson recruited two regiments of free Afro-Americans from Louisiana, offering them a bonus of $125 and 160 acres of land if they would serve in the army during the war with Great Britain. Their contribution to the defense of the area won the praise of their immediate superiors, General Jackson, and national leaders.

Great Britain also had black soldiers. In addition to Afro-Americans from the United States who defected to the British, there was also a black regiment from the West Indies that fought against General Jackson's Afro-American troops in the Battle of New Orleans.

As in the Revolutionary War, slaves were allowed to enlist in the army provided they had the written permission of their masters. Generally they were promised and therefore expected their freedom at the end of the hostilities. When the war ended, however, facts indicate that although some of the slaves were freed, others were either sent back to their masters or sold into slavery elsewhere.

REFERENCES

Nell, William C., *Services of Colored Americans in the Wars of 1776 and 1812* (Boston: Prentiss & Sawyer, 1851).

Wilkes, Laura E., *Missing Pages in American History* (Washington, D.C.: R. L. Pendleton, 1919).

Williams, George W., *A History of Negro Troops in the War of the Rebellion* (New York: G. P. Putnam's Sons, 1888).

Wilson, Joseph T., *The Black Phalanx; A History of Negro Soldiers in the Wars of 1776, 1812, and 1861-1865* (Hartford, Conn.: American Publishers Co., 1888).

10
Afro-American–Indian Relations

Throughout the history of the institution of slavery some Afro-Americans sought refuge with the Indians along the frontiers. The vast majority were fugitive slaves who had run away from their plantations. In addition there were free blacks who had migrated to the Indian settlements and also those Afro-Americans who were purchased by Indians as slaves.

Slave owners, especially in the South, frequently accused the Indians of harboring fugitive slaves and, partly for this reason, agitated for the removal of the Indians beyond the Mississippi River. This agitation was increased when the efforts to obtain fugitive slaves proved difficult, especially after Afro-Americans and Afro-American-Indians ("mustees" as they were called) became important factors in the Indian settlements. Seeking to reclaim fugitive slaves, whites sometimes raided Indian settlements. In addition to capturing fugitive slaves, they snatched away free Afro-Americans and mustees as well as Indian-owned slaves. Indians sought to reclaim those Afro-Americans who were rightfully settled in their communities, but being unaccustomed to such legal matters, they could not make a case before the courts, and even if they could, neither the Indians nor the blacks involved had any chance for justice.

These raids and injustices caused many battles between slave hunters and the Indians and Afro-Americans. The biggest and probably the best known in the United States was the Battle of Negro Fort in 1816, where the United States Army, after a bloody struggle, annihilated a large Afro-

American-Indian settlement in the Spanish territory of northwestern Florida. After this battle, the federal government, under every pretext, routed the Indians and acquired their land. By 1842 the United States Government had successfully relocated the Cherokees, Creeks, and most of the Seminoles west of the Mississippi River. The land thus acquired became an integral part of the Cotton Kingdom.

REFERENCES

Foreman, Grant, *Indian Removal: The Emigration of the Five Civilized Tribes of Indians* (Norman, Okla.: University of Oklahoma Press, 1932).
Porter, Kenneth W., "Relations Between Negroes and Indians Within the Present Limits of the United States," *Journal of Negro History*, XVII (July 1932).
_____, "Negroes and the Seminole War, 1835-1842," *Journal of Southern History*, XXX (November 1964).
_____, "Negroes and the Seminole War, 1817-1818," *Journal of Negro History*, XXXVI (July 1951).
_____, "Slaves and Free Negroes in the Seminole War, 1835-1842," *Journal of Negro History*, XXVIII (October 1943).

11
The Cotton Kingdom

The Cotton Kingdom began with the invention of the cotton gin. Without it cotton would have remained an unimportant crop in the South. The problem was the lack of an economical means of separating the cotton seed from the fiber, a process laboriously done by hand. Since a slave could clean only about one pound of short-staple cotton and ten pounds of the long-fibered variety in one day, the cost of producing cotton goods was very high. A machine had to be invented in order to make it less expensive. The job was done by Eli Whitney in 1793.

The invention of the cotton gin ushered in a period of economic change that was to alter radically the southern way of life. With the new gin slaves could clean 150 pounds of cotton a day, and later when steam was applied to the gin they could clean 1000 pounds per day. Four hundred times more cotton was produced by the South in 1860 than in 1793, and cotton became the foundation of the whole economic, political, and cultural life in the South as well as in much of the North.

Many small farmers of the South were adversely affected by the emergence of the Cotton Kingdom. They could not successfully compete with the large planters, and consequently many found themselves driven into unfertile mountainous areas or to the frontier. As a result some antislavery sentiment developed among this group of whites, but being deeply steeped in white supremacy prejudices, their opposition to the planter aristocracy was largely dissipated.

The Indians along the southern frontier were also adversely affected by the advance of the Cotton Kingdom. Under every plausible pretext, they were ruthlessly robbed of their valuable land by land speculators who received backing from both state and federal governments. The emergence of the Cotton Kingdom also had other effects:

1. It solidified the institution of slavery.
2. It made the question of slavery one of national importance.
3. It relegated the economy of the South to dependence on agriculture and northern capital.
4. It increased the demand for slaves and raised the value of those slaves already in the United States to greatly inflated prices.
5. It worked against the possibility of increased private manumissions.
6. It eventually raised cries for a resumption of the slave trade.
7. It encouraged much harsher exploitation of the slaves and thus nullified many of the ameliorating effects of growing humanitarian sentiment.

With the annexation of Texas in 1845, the slave empire of the South consisted of fifteen states ranging southward and westward from the Mason-Dixon Line to the Rio Grande River.

REFERENCES

Christy, David, *Cotton Is King* (Cincinnati: Moore, Wilstach, Keys & Co., 1855).
Dodd, William E., *The Cotton Kingdom* (New Haven, Conn.: Yale University Press, 1919).
Gray, Lewis C., *History of Agriculture in the Southern United States* (Washington, D.C.: Carnegie Institute of Washington, 1933).
May, Robert E., *The Southern Dream of a Caribbean Empire, 1854-1861* (Baton Rouge: Louisiana State University Press, 1973).
*Phillips, Ulrich B., *American Negro Slavery* (New York: D. Appleton & Co., 1918 [Louisiana State University Press]).
*Turner, Frederick J., *The Rise of the New West* (New York: Harper & Brothers, 1906 [Collier, Macmillan]).
*Weinberg, Albert K., *Manifest Destiny, A Study of Nationalist Expansionism in American History* (Baltimore, Md.: Johns Hopkins Press, 1935 [Quadrangle]).

12
Domestic Slave Trade

The domestic slave trade evolved along with the institution of slavery, and it became a tremendously profitable and active business after the invention of the cotton gin in 1793 and the outlawing of the African slave trade in 1808. Its growth was also aided by the depletion of the soil, especially in the upper South, and by the decrease in value of some of the cash crops that were grown along the southeastern seaboard and in the upper South.

The War of 1812 checked the growth of the domestic slave trade, but thereafter it flourished. The names of slave traders began to appear regularly in all of the newspapers and journals in the South. The principal domestic slave trading centers were Baltimore, Washington, D.C., Richmond, Norfolk, and Charleston. From these points slave traders would scour the countryside, gathering slaves for resale in the expanding cotton belt. In the slave trading centers the slaves were housed in private and public jails or slave pens to await sale. During the period of incarceration, the slaves were well fed and clothed in order to make them more salable.

Sales were both private and public, but at either type the slave was subjected to close inspection by the prospective purchaser. The prerequisites for a good price for a male field hand were youth and strength; for a skilled artisan or servant, reliability and skill; and for a woman, health and some indication of her ability to reproduce. The prices paid for slaves varied with the demand for them. At the peak of Cotton Kingdom expansion in the 1850s, it was not uncommon for a purchaser to pay from $1000 to

$2500 for a prime field hand or a young mulatto "wench" who was guaranteed to have reproductive qualities. After the sale the slaves were taken south by ship along the eastern seaboard or down the Mississippi River, by overland march, or by railroad.

Maryland and Virginia were almost exclusively slave-exporting states, with the Carolinas and Kentucky closely following. The states in the lower South—Florida, Arkansas, Georgia, Alabama, Mississippi, Louisiana, and Texas—were almost exclusively importing states.

REFERENCES

Bancroft, Frederic, *Slave Trading in the Old South* (Baltimore, Md.: J. H. Furst Co., 1931).

Campbell, Stanley W., *The Slave Catchers: Enforcement of the Fugitive Slave Law 1850-60* (Chapel Hill: University of North Carolina Press, 1970).

Carey, Henry C., *The Slave Trade, Domestic and Foreign: Why It Exists and How It May Be Extinguished* (Philadelphia: H. C. Baird, 1872).

LaPrade, William T., "The Domestic Slave Trade in the District of Columbia," *Journal of Negro History*, XI (January 1926).

13
The Slave "Family"

The slave family was very unstable because the forces inherent in the American system of slavery worked against its stability. With few exceptions, slave marriages were not legally required, slave fatherhood was not legally recognized, legal prohibitions against dividing slave families were uncommon and where they did exist they were conveniently ignored, customary "courtship" and "engagement" seldom existed, and many slave owners were very reluctant to allow "marriages" between slaves who lived on different plantations.

Whatever recognition the slave family received was voluntary on the part of the master. A few owners insisted on religious ceremonies to unite slave couples, and other owners informally sanctioned the relationship of slave couples. In addition, where there were children involved, the slave family sometimes tended to be more stable, and a few states had laws forbidding the selling of mothers away from their children who were under a certain age. However, this did not apply to fathers. It should be recognized that in all cases where the maintenance of a stable family was detrimental to the economic interest of the master, the slave family was inevitably divided. Wives would be sold away from their husbands and children, husbands from their wives and children, and children from their parents, brothers, and sisters.

Because of the difficulty in establishing and maintaining a "normal" stable slave family, cohabitation, sometimes forced, was widespread. In such cases a close family relationship had little chance to develop, for very seldom did the parties want or have time to learn to care for each other. Children of such relationships also suffered the pangs of nonaffection, since their parents, especially the mother, had little time for child-rearing and in many instances she was largely relieved of this responsibility. However, whenever possible the slave mother did everything she could to maintain a stable family, and she grieved very deeply when the family was divided.

Despite laws against it, miscegenation was extensive, especially between white men and slave women. Slave women had no rights and few means to protect themselves against the sexual desires of white men. Concubinage and polygamy were so widespread in some cities in the South that they almost gained social acceptance. The rape of a slave woman was not a crime but merely a trespass on the property of her master. Children of such relationships were slaves and were generally treated accordingly. In a few instances, however, white fathers emancipated them and provided for them. The extent of such miscegenous relationships is evidenced by the mulatto slave population, which in 1860 was estimated to be 410,000 out of a total slave population of approximately 4,000,000. The proportion of mulattoes among the "free" Afro-American population was considerably higher.

Slave breeding also contributed to the instability of the slave family. The prohibition of the African slave trade after 1808, the decline in the value of certain cash crops, the deterioration of the soil in the upper South, and the expansion of the Cotton Kingdom all made slave breeding inevitable. It had existed to a small extent since the beginning of the institution of slavery in North America, but after the turn of the nineteenth century, when the demand for slaves reached its peak, slave breeding became a common means of gaining profit, especially in the states of the upper South.

Slaves, male and female, were purchased especially for breeding purposes. Sometimes no regard was paid to the preferences of slaves in matters of mating, but generally slave owners preferred to let slaves pick their own mates since this made the slaves more "contented" and more likely to produce offspring. Breeding slaves were pampered, well fed and clothed, and treated less brutally. They were generally not overworked; in fact some were given bounties at the birth of each child, and occasionally women were emancipated if they gave birth to a specified number of children.

In view of the instability of the slave family and the almost total absence of slave marriages, the slave woman tended to become the head of the family, for it was she who provided what little degree of stability that existed in the "home." One fact of slavery that has not yet been adequately treated in the literature is the heroic efforts on the part of slave fathers and mothers to maintain stable family relationships despite impossible odds. That many of them succeeded is a most remarkable aspect of the black experience in America. And the fact that the overwhelming majority of black families have achieved stability in a short span of one hundred years suggests that the abolition of slavery, more than any other social act, contributed to this stability. It also suggests that the best way to further enhance the stability of black families would be to abolish all the remaining vestiges of bondage black people now experience in this country.[*]

REFERENCES

Bancroft, Frederic, *Slave Trading in the Old South* (Baltimore, Md.: J. H. Furst Co., 1931).

*Billingsley, A., *Black Families in White America* (Englewood Cliffs, N.J.: Prentice-Hall, Inc., 1968 [Prentice-Hall]).

Blassingame, John W., *The Slave Community: Plantation Life in the Ante-Bellum South* (New York: Oxford University Press, 1972).

Bontemps, Arna, *Great Slave Narratives* (Boston: Beacon Press, 1969).

Cobbs, H., A. Grier, and M. Price, *Black Rage* (New York: Basic Books, 1968).

Fogel, Robert W., and Stanley L. Engerman, *Time on the Cross* (Boston: Little, Brown, and Company, 1974).

Frazier, E. Franklin, *The Negro Family in the United States* (Chicago: The University of Chicago Press, 1966).

Gray, Lewis C., *History of Agriculture in the Southern United States to 1860* (Washington, D.C.: Carnegie Institute of Washington, 1933).

*Phillips, Ulrich B., *American Negro Slavery* (New York: D. Appleton & Co., 1918 [Louisiana State University Press]).

*Stampp, Kenneth M., *The Peculiar Institution* (New York: Knopf, Random House, 1956 [Vintage]).

[*]Robert W. Fogel and Stanley L. Engerman, employing computers and other complex mathematical techniques, compiled and analyzed masses of what was hitherto thought of as unusable data and reached strikingly different interpretations and conclusions about the peculiar institution. In *Time on the Cross* these econometric historians allege that slave family life was encouraged, that most slaves were diligent and effective workers, and that the material conditions of slaves was comparable to that of industrial workers.

14
Antebellum Slavery

It is estimated that the slave population of the United States was less than 700,000 in 1790. By 1830 there were more than two million slaves, and in the early 1860s the number of slaves had soared to approximately four million. During antebellum times, the slave population of the lower South was increasing rapidly, while that of the upper South was either increasing very slowly or decreasing. Over half of the slave population was employed in agriculture, and the vast majority of these were employed in the production of cotton. The remainder were employed in the production of tobacco, rice, sugar, and hemp. In 1860 the white population of the South numbered approximately eight million. However, there were only 385,885 owners of slaves, and 88 percent of these owned less than twenty slaves. The planter aristocracy, those owning more than one hundred slaves, numbered less than three thousand white families.

PLANTATION LIFE

The plantation and the farm were the typical locale of the slave. Where there were few slaves, they and their owner worked together in the fields. On the large farms and plantations there was direct supervision by the owner or his overseer, but the majority of the plantations were managed by the planters themselves.

The overseer was a white male hired by the owner to supervise the daily administration of the plantation. He was employed by written contract on a year-to-year basis. He was paid an annual salary and was furnished a house, an allowance of food, and a slave servant. His duties were generally set forth in writing and related to the care and control of the slaves, the amount and kinds of labor to be performed, the care of the plantation tools and livestock, and his own behavior. He was also required to keep a written, daily record of the plantation activities and to make regular reports to the owner. The overseer's performance rarely satisfied the planter. He was accused of and was more often than not guilty of neglect of the tools and livestock, inhumane treatment of the slaves, or general inefficiency. His tenure averaged two to three years at each plantation.

On the larger plantations the overseer made use of one or more slaves who were chosen to become a part of the plantation hierarchy. These slaves, called drivers, were responsible for maintaining order and discipline on the plantation and for supervising the tasks assigned to slaves under their direction. For this they received larger portions of food, clothes, or other rewards. The drivers reported every evening to the overseer on the employment of their hands and received instructions for the following day.

The most important worker on the plantation was the field hand. On an agricultural unit where there were no house servants, field hands performed household chores as well as their duties in the fields. There tended to be labor specialization on plantations with large numbers of slaves, where distinction was made between house servants and field hands. Field hands devoted full time to plowing, hoeing, ditching, tending livestock, ginning, and weeding. Domestic slaves served as cooks, body servants, coachmen, and maids.

For the field hands, the day's toil began at sunrise and ended at dusk. There were two rest periods, when breakfast and lunch were eaten in the fields. Dinner was eaten at the slave quarters after the slaves returned for the night. Night work was uncommon on most plantations except during harvest, when the slaves were compelled by many masters to work from sixteen to eighteen hours a day, seven days a week, without rest periods. During nonharvest times the slaves worked only a half day on Saturday, and they were off all day Sunday.

Field hands were generally overworked, especially when they were under the supervision of an overseer whose salary and reemployment depended on the size of the crop. Where the owner worked in the fields with his slaves, there was likely to be less brutality. But no matter who was supervising the field labor, when there was not close supervision of the slaves, little work was accomplished, for they felt no compulsion to extend themselves unless forced to do so. Slaves did prove more willing to work, however, in those cases where masters chose to offer rewards for good productivity.

The type of labor system used to achieve a maximum harvest depended primarily upon the crop raised, but basically there were two types of systems used in working the field hands—the gang system and the task system, the first being based on a certain number of hours and the second on the amount of work done. Rewards and bounties were also offered to achieve maximum production. The number of acres each field hand was expected to cultivate depended upon how hard the master or overseer wished to work him, the nature of the soil, the quality of the tools, and the crop itself. The prime field hand was expected to cultivate at least three acres of cotton a season, and other slaves—children, women, breeders, and aged or infirm slaves—were expected to cultivate proportionately less. The food rations that the field hands received were meager. Either once a week or daily they received a portion of meal and salt pork, which at times was supplemented with sweet potatoes, peas, rice, syrup, and fruit. In addition, slaves had what they grew in their own gardens (if permitted to keep them), what they could steal from the master's storehouse, and what they hunted and fished (if permitted to).

The slaves who were valued most highly on a plantation were those who had acquired special skills. This group included engineers, coopers, carpenters, blacksmiths, bricklayers, stonemasons, mechanics, and others. Their lot was much better than that of the field hand. They were better clothed and fed, and their hours of labor were not as long. Also, many skilled slaves had the opportunity to hire themselves out during their own time.

Domestic servants were prized almost as much as skilled slaves. The number and variety of domestics in a household depended upon the size of the plantation and the wealth of the master. Like the skilled slave, they were generally better fed and clothed than the field hand. Their hours were shorter and their tasks less strenuous. However, during harvest time, domestic slaves often worked in the fields.

Slaves were given clothes once a year. There were shirts and blue jeans for the men and calico shifts for the women. Children were permitted to go naked until they were six or seven years old. Domestics were better clothed, for they received "hand-me-downs" from the master and mistress of the "big house." The housing for slaves was inadequate: Each dwelling was small and ill constructed, with no windows, bare walls, and without furnishings. Generally it was located some distance from the "big house." There was little in the way of social life for the slaves during the moments they were off the job. They worked such long and hard hours that periods of free time had to be used for rest. When the opportunity for diversion did present itself (holidays, races, fairs, and elections) slaves would fish, hunt, visit, or otherwise tend to their personal needs. Often there was opportunity to attend church on Sunday.

NONAGRICULTURAL PURSUITS

In 1860 approximately a half million slaves were engaged in work not directly related to agriculture. They were located in cities, towns, and labor camps throughout the South. These slaves worked in the turpentine industry, in sawmills, quarries, and fisheries, and as lumberjacks. They mined coal, salt, lead, and iron. On riverboats they were pilots, deckhands, and firemen, and they also worked on the construction and maintenance of roads, railroads, and canals. Slaves virtually monopolized the domestic services, and they were also to be found at cotton gins, sugar refineries, tanneries, shipyards, bakehouses, laundries, and the few factories in the South.

SLAVES FOR HIRE

One day of each year was designated when masters with slaves to spare and employers in search of labor bargained for the rental of slaves. Some of the hirings were negotiated privately, some by auctioneers, and some by agents who handled the transaction for a commission. Though slaves were occasionally hired for short terms, it was the customary practice to hire them for a year. Written contracts specified the period of hire, the kind of work that the slaves were to be engaged in, the hirer's obligation to keep them well clothed and fed, and the amount of money involved. Potential hirers were generally small farmers who needed extra hands during harvest time, railroad companies, construction companies, shipyards, and others who needed laborers for a specified period of time.

Slaves who were skilled laborers sometimes had the opportunity to hire themselves out on their own time, or they might be hired out by their masters. These slaves were required to pay their masters a specified sum of money and could retain the remainder. These slaves enjoyed considerable freedom, and some were even able to purchase their own freedom.

BLACK CODES

After the establishment of the federal government, the individual states wasted no time passing laws with reference to the Afro-American. While the northern states were fast putting an end to the institution of slavery, the slave codes remained operative in the South where the institution was becoming firmly entrenched in every aspect of life.

As the slave population increased, more and more laws were passed to insure complete protection of whites against slave revolts or other misconduct. Like their predecessors, the Black Codes were repressive and contained many restrictions: Slaves had no standing in court, they could not enter into contracts, they could not own property, they could not strike a white person or treat a white person with disrespect, they could not leave the plantation without written authorization, they could not own or possess firearms, they could not conduct themselves as free, they could not assemble with other slaves without either permission or the presence of a white man, and they could not consume or purchase alcoholic beverages. These are only a few of the restrictions that governed the slave's economic, social, political, and civil life.

Whenever there was a revolt or the rumor of one, there was a tendency to enforce existing laws brutally and to enact more laws to further control the slave's activities and movements. At other times the codes were only nominally enforced.

THE SLAVE'S VIEW OF SLAVERY

Slaves, whether field hands, domestic servants, or skilled artisans, knew that the institution of slavery was a system of human exploitation. The brutality that was inherent in the system existed in every antebellum community, and slaves reacted accordingly. In their attempts to lessen their burden, slaves limited the quantity and quality of their work. They damaged property, they abused livestock, they injured crops, they idled in the slave quarters or on the job, they feigned illness, they maimed or mutilated themselves, they committed suicide, they committed infanticide, they committed personal acts of violence, and they ran away. The most desperate reaction of slaves to their status was the attempt to revolt. Revolts or conspiracies to revolt began with the institution of slavery and did not end until slavery was abolished, but it was during the antebellum era that the entire South was most apprehensive about uprisings. Virginia and South Carolina experienced major uprisings. Sadly the revolts usually resulted in a loss of lives, both white and particularly Afro-American.

It should be realized that no expression of discontent, whether by a single slave or by a group, had a chance of destroying the institution of slavery: Slaves lacked the power to do so. But by lashing out at slavery the slaves provided ample evidence to refute the apologists' arguments that the institution was paternalistic and that the slaves enjoyed their lot in blissful contentment.

REFERENCES

*Elkins, Stanley, *Slavery: A Problem in American Institutional and Intellectual Life* (Chicago: University of Chicago Press, 1959 [University of Chicago Press]).

Genovese, Eugene D., *Roll, Jordan, Roll: The World the Slaves Made* (New York: Pantheon Books, 1974).

Gray, Lewis C., *History of Agriculture in the Southern United States to 1860* (Washington, D.C.: Carnegie Institute of Washington, 1933).

Olmstead, Frederick L., *The Cotton Kingdom: A Traveller's Observations on Cotton and Slavery in the American Slave States* (New York: Knopf, 1953).

*Phillips, Ulrich B., *Life and Labor in the Old South* (Boston: Little, Brown & Co., 1963 [ALB, Little]).

Scarborough, William K., *The Overseer: Plantation Management in the Old South* (Baton Rouge, La.: Louisiana State University Press, 1966).

*Stampp, Kenneth M., *The Peculiar Institution: Slavery in the Antebellum South* (New York: Knopf, Random House, 1956 [Vintage]).

*Wade, Richard L., *Slavery in the Cities: The South, 1820-1860* (New York: Oxford University Press, 1964 [Oxford University Press]).

Wilson, Theodore B., *The Black Codes of the South* (University, Ala.: University of Alabama Press, 1965).

15
Slavery: Pro and Con

IN DEFENSE OF SLAVERY

During and after the Revolutionary War slaveholders either denounced slavery, were silent, or shamefacedly defended it as a "necessary evil." But with the development of King Cotton and in the face of northern attacks on the institution, they began to advocate slavery as "a positive good." Even when abolitionism was at its peak and the institution was being attacked on political, social, economic, and humanitarian grounds, slaveocrats made it very clear that the institution was vital to the southern way of life and that they would defend it at any cost. They argued that:

1. The prosperity of the South depended on slave labor.
2. Afro-Americans were destined to occupy a subordinate position in society because they were biologically inferior.
3. The Old and the New Testaments sanctioned slavery.
4. Without slavery whites would not be able to develop or maintain a high degree of culture.
5. Slavery was more benevolent than the "wage slavery" of the North.

Pro-slavery advocates did not limit their defense to philosophical arguments. They defended their "peculiar" institution physically. Persons with points of view at variance with the pro-slavery creed were run out of the

South. Churches, colleges, and social, civil, cultural, and political organizations were employed to defend slavery. Whites who suggested abolition of the institution were publicly whipped or even put to death, and persons suspected of being abolitionists or agents in the Underground Railroad were similarly dealt with. Leaders in the abolitionist movement had prices on their heads. Abolitionist literature was seized and burned. Nor did pro-slavery advocates limit their activities to the South: They went north and west, making speeches and passing out literature in defense of the institution. They even attempted to infiltrate the abolitionist movement in an effort to learn how the Underground Railroad operated.

On the eve of the Civil War, abolitionists in the North and West had resolved to destroy slavery by one means or another, and pro-slavery advocates in the South had resolved to maintain their "peculiar" institution at all costs.

THE ABOLITIONIST MOVEMENT

Shortly after the end of the Revolutionary War, the antislavery philosophy that had been so clearly proclaimed during the hostilities began to weaken. Yet it never completely died out. To be sure, there was a period of quiescence, but even during these times prominent citizens, local organizations, and even state legislatures debated the pros and cons of the institution of slavery and weighed programs of emancipation.

About 1830 antislavery sentiment suddenly increased. In 1829 David Walker, a free Afro-American, published his "Appeal," a militant call upon slaves to throw off the chains of slavery. In 1831 William Lloyd Garrison began publication of *The Liberator*, a newspaper advancing an unprecedented brand of unequivocal abolitionism. These publications coincided with the Nat Turner rebellion of 1831. The age of the militant abolitionist had arrived. What heretofore had been pleas for gradual emancipation or emancipation with compensation or colonization became demands for immediate emancipation. Abolitionists, Afro-American and white, worked out elaborate arguments against the institution of slavery. They insisted that it was contrary to the teachings of Christianity, the libertarian principles of the American way of life, and the brotherhood of man. They contended that it was economically unsound and a threat to peace.

With these principles abolitionists throughout the nation met and formed the American Antislavery Society in 1833. The Society published books, pamphlets, and leaflets, distributing them throughout the nation.

Through its many agents, local branches were established and money was raised to further the program of immediate emancipation. Lectures were given, rallies held, and debates conducted. Militant abolitionists soon became impatient with the slow progress being made by the American Antislavery Society. They believed that there should be immediate emancipation at any cost—even war. As a result, and owing also to disagreement as to whether women should participate in the movement on an equal basis with men, the American and Foreign Antislavery Society was formed in 1840 by those who believed that emancipation could be brought about by moral persuasion and political action. After the split in the abolitionist forces the effective work was done largely by state and local organizations.

In 1840, a new national political party appeared on the scene, the Liberty Party. It resulted from a split between the pro- and anti-political factions in the American Antislavery Society. The Party demanded an end of slavery in the District of Columbia, it called for disobedience to the Fugitive Slave Act of 1793, and it opposed the expansion of slavery into new territories. Many Afro-American leaders supported the Liberty Party, and a few were, for the first time in United States history, nominated for national and state offices on the ticket of a national political party. The Liberty Party is of historical significance because it was the first national political party to carry the matter of the abolition of slavery into the political arena. In 1848 the Liberty Party abolitionists, Free Soil Whigs, and "Barnburners" merged into the Free Soil Party.

Afro-Americans played a significant role in the abolitionist movement. From the inception of the institution of slavery, they spoke out loudly against its evils. They aided in the establishment of state and local antislavery societies, and they could be found in the ranks of national antislavery organizations, including the American Antislavery Society, the American and Foreign Antislavery Society, and the Negro Convention Movement. They served as organizers, lecturers, and pamphleteers. Outstanding among the Afro-American abolitionists was Frederick Douglass, an escaped slave, who became one of the most brilliant writers and orators of his day.

Nothing did more to emphasize the determination of the abolitionists to destroy slavery than the Underground Railroad. Slaves generally began their trip on the plantation and followed one of many roads across rivers, valleys, and mountains leading to freedom in the North or Canada. In many cases the slaves were aided in this dangerous journey by "conductors" who guided them safely along the way. At the "stations" along the route to freedom the slaves received food and lodging. Of the abolitionists engaged in spiriting slaves to safety, the most outstanding was Harriet Tubman who reportedly made no less than nineteen trips to the South, bringing out approximately 300 slaves. Her work was so effective that slaveholders posted a reward of $40,000 for her, dead or alive. There is no way of determining the exact number of slaves who escaped via the Underground Railroad, but one historian indicates that between 1810 and 1850 the South lost approximately 100,000 slaves through this means.

REFERENCES

Adams, Alice D., *The Neglected Period of Antislavery in America, 1808-1831* (Boston: Ginn & Co., 1908).

Aptheker, Herbert, "Militant Abolitionism," *Journal of Negro History*, XXVI (October 1941).

———, *The Negro in the Abolitionist Movement* (New York: International Publishers, Inc., 1941).

*Barnes, Gilbert H., *The Antislavery Impulse, 1830-1844* (New York: D. Appleton & Co., 1933 [Harcourt, Brace & World, Inc.]).

———, and Dwight L. Dumond, eds., *Letters of Theodore Dwight Weld, Angelina Grimke Weld, and Sarah Grimke, 1822-1844* (New York: D. Appleton & Co., 1934).

Buckmaster, Henrietta, *Let My People Go* (Boston: Beacon Press, 1959).

Carpenter, Jesse, *The South as a Conscious Minority, 1789-1861* (New York: New York University Press, 1930).

*Douglass, Frederick, *The Life and Times of Frederick Douglass* (Cambridge, Mass.: Belknap Press, 1960 [Collier, Macmillan]).

*Duberman, Martin, ed., *The Antislavery Vanguard: New Essays on the Abolitionists* (Princeton, N.J.: Princeton University Press, 1965).

*Dumond, Dwight L., *Antislavery: The Crusade for Freedom in America* (Ann Arbor, Mich.: University of Michigan Press, 1961 [Norton]).

*Eaton, Clement, *Freedom of Thought in the Old South* (Durham, N.C.: Duke University Press, 1940 [Harper & Row]).

*Filler, Louis, *The Crusade Against Slavery, 1830-1860* (New York: Harper & Row, 1960 [Torchbook, Harper & Row]).

Fladeland, Betty, *Men and Brothers: Anglo-American Antislavery Cooperation* (Urbana: University of Illinois, 1972).

*Gara, Larry, *The Liberty Line: The Legend of the Underground Railroad* (Lexington, Ky.: University of Kentucky Press, 1961 [University of Kentucky Press]).

Hesseltine, W. B., "Some New Aspects of the Pro-Slavery Argument," *Journal of Negro History*, XXI (January 1936).

Jenkins, William S., *Pro-Slavery Thought in the Old South* (Chapel Hill, N.C.: University of North Carolina Press, 1935).

Locke, Mary S., *Antislavery in America from the Introduction of African Slaves to the Prohibition of the Slave Trade (1619-1808)* (Boston: Ginn & Co., 1901).

*McKitrick, Eric L., *Slavery Defended: The Views of the Old South* (Englewood Cliffs, N.J.: Prentice-Hall, 1963 [Prentice-Hall]).

Morrow, Ralph E., "The Pro-Slavery Argument Revisited," *Mississippi Valley Historical Review*, XLVIII (June 1961).

Siebert, Wilbur H., *The Underground Railroad from Slavery to Freedom* (New York: The Macmillan Co., 1898).

*Stanton, William R., *The Leopard's Spots: Scientific Attitudes Toward Race in America, 1815-1859* (Chicago: The University of Chicago Press, 1960 [Phoenix, The University of Chicago Press]).

Still, William, *The Underground Railroad* (Philadelphia: Porter & Coates, 1872).

Takaki, Ronald T., *A Pro-Slavery Crusade: The Agitation to Reopen the African Slave Trade* (New York: The Free Press, 1971).

Thomas, John L., *The Liberator: William Lloyd Garrison* (Boston: Little, Brown and Co., 1963).

Woodson, Carter G., ed., *The Mind of the Negro as Reflected in Letters During the Crisis, 1800-1860* (Washington, D.C.: Association for the Study of Negro Life & History, 1926).

16
The Civil War

PRELUDE: THE PERIOD OF INTERSECTIONAL STRIFE

When the Constitutional Convention met in 1787, to be sure, some delegates representing the commercial interests of the North clashed with delegates representing the planter interest of the South on several sectional questions regarding the institution of slavery and the slave trade, but sectional controversies were of secondary importance. With the passage of time, however, sectional interests became clear-cut. During the 1790s planters constantly pointed out that northern manufacturers were the only ones benefiting from federal legislation. Moreover, Southerners knew that it was only a matter of time before the North would be in complete control of the federal government.

Seeing their power declining and their institutions under attack, Southerners realized that something had to be done. If no agreement could be reached with the North on the slavery question, the formation of two confederacies would be inevitable. Between 1820 and 1861, the country witnessed a series of crises that resulted in the Civil War. Some of the more important controversies that widened the gulf between the northern and southern states were:

1. The Missouri Compromise of 1820
2. The solidification of the abolitionist movement during the 1830s
3. The Nullification Controversy and the Tariff Compromise of 1833
4. The annexation of Texas in 1845
5. The formation of the Free Soil Party in 1848
6. The Compromise of 1850
7. The publication of *Uncle Tom's Cabin* in 1852
8. The Kansas-Nebraska Bill of 1854
9. The formation of the Republican Party of 1854
10. The Dred Scott decision of 1857
11. John Brown's raid in 1859
12. The election of Abraham Lincoln in 1860

WAR COMMENCES

The Civil War commenced on April 12, 1861. On the same day Lincoln called for volunteers, and Afro-Americans were not inattentive. In the North Afro-Americans formed drill companies and presented their services, but the state and federal governments declined their offers. Free Afro-Americans of the South also offered their services to the Confederacy, but they too were turned away. A few Afro-Americans, north and south, attached themselves to the armed forces and performed domestic or fatigue duties.

IN THE UNION ARMY

As the Union Armies advanced, the problem arose as to what should be done with the thousands of slaves who were flocking to the Union lines. Because there was no federal policy, field generals had to make their own decisions. Some turned the fugitives away; some allowed slave hunters to enter their lines and recapture them; some designated the runaways as contraband, refused to return them, and put them to work; some issued deeds manumitting the former slaves, but these deeds were generally countermanded. Contraband slaves served very useful purposes: They brought unrivaled knowledge of the South's waterways and countryside; they brought information regarding the Confederate military posture; they served the Union forces as scouts and spies; and they supplied the bulk of the labor, building forts, roads, bridges, etc.

With the successful utilization of the runaway slaves and the critical manpower shortages, the agitation for arming Afro-Americans increased. Without orders several Union generals in the South had, on their own, formed Afro-American regiments from among the runaways, but these had to be disbanded because of the federal government's "do nothing" policy in this regard.

In the North pressure was also growing to use Afro-Americans as soldiers. State governors who had initially refused their services were now compelled to muster them in, for they were not able to meet their enlistment quotas and several northern states were threatened with invasion by the Confederate Army. Under these circumstances Lincoln issued the Emancipation Proclamation that, along with freeing the slaves in those states or parts thereof that were still in rebellion, permitted freed slaves of suitable condition into the armed services. Shortly thereafter authorizations were sent to the state governors—and to individuals, where state officials refused to act—authorizing the recruitment of Negroes. On April 29, 1865, when the recruitment of Afro-Americans was terminated, the Bureau of Colored Troops reported 166 Afro-American regiments—145 infantry, 7 cavalry, 12 heavy artillery, 1 light artillery, and 1 engineer. More than 186,000 men, approximately one-eighth of those serving in the Union Army, were Afro-Americans.

Afro-American soldiers faced many problems:

1. The names of their regiments had to include the word "colored."
2. They operated under a guide entitled "United States Infantry Tactics for the Use of Colored Troops."
3. They were seldom commissioned as officers during the war (the commissioned officers in Afro-American units were almost always whites).
4. They were paid less than white soldiers until 1864.
5. They received inferior hospital care and consequently suffered a 40 percent higher mortality rate than did white soldiers.
6. They were given inferior guns and other essential equipment.
7. They were assigned an excessive amount of fatigue duty.
8. They were not considered prisoners of war if captured by the Confederacy until 1864, and therefore they were not included in prisoner exchanges.
9. They were socially discriminated against.

Even in the face of numerous difficulties, the Afro-American was a good soldier and performed courageously. From Port Hudson, the first real battle in which Afro-American soldiers were engaged, to Appomattox, they served gallantly, for they knew that a Union victory meant freedom. Afro-American women also played an important role on the battlefield. They served as spies and scouts, as hospital attendants, cooks, nurses, and in other noncombatant roles.

IN THE UNION NAVY

Afro-Americans also served in the Union Navy. Throughout its history the Navy had never barred Afro-Americans from enlisting and, suffering from a manpower shortage during the course of the war, it encouraged their enlistment. Segregation and discrimination were at a minimum, and in prisoner exchanges no question of color ever came up. Afro-Americans served in all capacities in the Navy. There were a few senior ship officers. It is estimated that out of 118,044 enlistments in the Navy during the Civil War, 29,511 were Afro-Americans. They served with valor, for they too knew that a Union victory meant freedom for the slaves.

NORTHERN AFRO-AMERICAN CIVILIANS

By mid-1863 the fear of competition of the Afro-American laborer had reached a high pitch. In a few instances the contrabands were working in jobs that whites had vacated in order to serve in the Union Armies. But the widespread belief that slaves, if liberated, would overrun the North was totally unfounded. In an effort to reduce Afro-American competition, the white workers resorted to all-white unions and to mob violence in many northern cities. The fear of white longshoremen, who were drafted after they struck for higher wages, that Afro-Americans would permanently replace them on the docks was a major factor leading to the New York draft riots of 1863.

In the face of many hazards northern Afro-Americans aided the Union cause. They worked in factories and along the docks, and they served as recruiters and fund raisers.

AFRO-AMERICAN SERVICE
TO THE CONFEDERACY

In the initial stages of the war, free Afro-Americans offered their service, but there was widespread opposition. A few attached themselves to the Confederate Army doing noncombatant chores, while others contributed money, materials, and foodstuffs.

Some Afro-Americans were faithful to their masters and to the Confederacy throughout the war. These were generally house servants and body servants of Confederate Army officers who were sincerely attached to their masters. But a great many more slaves evinced an unwillingness to work and a novel insolence. Running away became more common, and in every locality the approach of the Union Army was accompanied by wholesale desertions from plantations. When they could, slaves in large numbers headed for the Union lines.

As the war continued, the importance of Afro-Americans to the Confederacy was realized. They produced its crops and manned its factories. So pressing was the need for military labor that the Confederate Congress was forced to pass impressment laws authorizing Confederate governors and Army officials to seize slaves and put them to work doing fatigue labor for which their owners would be compensated. The laws did not work well, however, for many slaves and owners were not inclined to cooperate.

CONFEDERATE POLICY REGARDING
ARMING AFRO-AMERICANS

Proposals to arm Afro-Americans, free and slave, came early in the war but were summarily rejected. By autumn 1863, the subject was openly debated as the Confederacy was faced with a critical manpower shortage. (In truth, the South was faced with a dilemma—to maintain the relationship of master to servant with the mythical justification of superior and inferior beings, or to arm Afro-Americans and thereby admit their equality.)

In late 1864, the Confederate governors passed a resolution recommending the use of slaves as soldiers. Under this pressure the Confederate Congress passed a law, which had the support of General Robert E. Lee, authorizing the arming of slaves. The bill was stillborn, for shortly thereafter, in April 1865, the Civil War ended.

REFERENCES

Aptheker, Herbert, *The Negro in the Civil War* (New York: International Publishers, Inc., 1938).

Brown, William Wells, *The Negro in the American Rebellion* (Boston: Lee & Shepard, 1867).

*Cornish, Dudley T., *The Sable Arm: Negro Troops in the Union Army, 1861-1865* (New York: Longmans, Green and Co., 1956 [Norton]).

Delany, Martin R., *The Condition, Elevation, Emigration, and Destiny of the Colored People of the United States, Politically Considered* (Philadelphia: The Author, 1852).

*Freehling, William, *Prelude to the Civil War: The Nullification Controversy in South Carolina, 1816-1836* (New York: Harper & Row, 1966 [Torchbook, Harper & Row]).

*Green, Fletcher M., *Constitutional Development in the South Atlantic States, 1776-1860* (Chapel Hill, N.C.: University of North Carolina Press, 1930 [Norton]).

Guthrie, James M., *Campfires of the Afro-American* (Philadelphia: Afro-American Publishing Co., 1899).

*Helper, Hinton R., *The Impending Crisis of the South: How to Meet It* (New York: Burdick Bros., 1857 [Macmillan; Harvard University Press]).

*Higginson, Thomas W., *Army Life in a Black Regiment* (East Lansing, Mich.: Michigan State University Press, 1960 [Macmillan]).

Lloyd, Arthur Y., *The Slavery Controversy, 1831-1860* (Chapel Hill, N.C.: University of North Carolina Press, 1939).

*McPherson, James M., *The Negro's Civil War: How American Negroes Felt and Acted During the War for the Union* (New York: Pantheon Books, 1965 [Random House]).

Nevins, Alan, *The War for the Union*, 2 vols. (New York: Charles Scribner's Sons, 1959-1960).

*Phillips, Ulrich B., *The Course of the South to Secession* (New York: D. Appleton & Co., 1939 [Hill & Wang]).

*Potter, David, *Lincoln and His Party in the Secession Crisis* (New Haven, Conn.: Yale University Press, 1942 [Yale University Press]).

Quarles, Benjamin, *Lincoln and the Negro* (New York: Oxford University Press, 1962).

_____, *The Negro in the Civil War* (Boston: Little, Brown and Co., 1953).

*Rhodes, James, *History of the United States from the Compromise of 1850* (New York: The Macmillan Co., 1893-1928 [The University of Chicago Press]).

Simms, Henry H., *A Decade of Sectional Controversy, 1851-1861* (Chapel Hill, N.C.: University of North Carolina Press, 1942).

*Stampp, Kenneth M., *And the War Came: The North and the Secession Crisis, 1860-1861* (Baton Rouge, La.: Louisiana State University Press [The University of Chicago Press]).

*Stowe, Harriet Beecher, *Uncle Tom's Cabin* (London: T. Bosworth, 1852 [Harper & Row]).

Welsey, Charles H., "The Civil War and the Negro American," *Journal of Negro History*, XLVII (April 1962).

*Wiley, Bell, *Southern Negroes, 1861-1865* (New Haven, Conn.: Yale University Press, 1965 [Yale University Press]).

Williams, George Washington, *History of the Negro Troops in the War of the Rebellion, 1861-1865* (New York: Harper & Bros., 1887).

Wilson, Joseph T., *The Black Phalanx: A History of Negro Soldiers in the Wars of 1776, 1812, and 1861-1865* (Hartford, Conn.: American Publishers Co., Inc., 1888).

17
The Reconstruction Era

LINCOLN'S SCHEME OF RECONSTRUCTION

From the early days of the Civil War the question of southern reconstruction was considered. Lincoln believed that the matter was one that should be handled by the President, and he informally suggested means by which southern Unionists could form loyal state governments and be readmitted to the Union. By the end of 1863 Lincoln saw the need for a definitive reconstruction plan, and on December 8, 1863, he issued a proclamation of amnesty and reconstruction. It stated that after one-tenth of the number of voters who voted in 1860 took an oath of allegiance, they could reorganize a state government. Only a limited number of Confederate military officials were denied the right to vote and hold office. Property rights were to be restored, except to own slaves. Afro-Americans were to be denied the right to vote.

Lincoln's reconstruction plan provoked opposition in Congress, the result of which was the passage of the Wade-Davis bill in July 1864. Radicals felt that the matter of reconstruction was solely a congressional matter. The bill contained severe restrictions regarding the right of ex-rebels to vote and hold office, it provided for provisional governors in the rebellious territories, it prohibited slavery, and it demanded the repudiation of war debts by the states. The bill did not provide franchise for Afro-Americans.

Lincoln vetoed the bill and in reaction the Wade-Davis manifesto was issued. It assailed Lincoln as a dictator and declared that he should confine himself to his executive duties ". . . to obey and execute, not make, the laws." The states of Virginia, Tennessee, Louisiana, and Arkansas formed loyal state governments under Lincoln's scheme of reconstruction, but they were never recognized by the Congress.

JOHNSON'S SCHEME OF RECONSTRUCTION

Because Johnson actively opposed secession, condemned the assassins of Lincoln, and worked closely with the Radical Republicans, it was assumed that he would carry out the Radicals' conception of reconstruction. The Radicals were disillusioned. On May 29, 1865, Johnson issued his amnesty proclamation whereby all persons who had participated in the rebellion, save certain groups, would have all their rights and properties, except slaves, restored to them upon taking a loyalty pledge. On the same day Johnson proclaimed his plan for reconstructing the Confederate state governments.

In each of the southern states, the President would appoint a provisional governor whose duty it would be to call a state convention and supervise the election of delegates to it. Only those who could qualify under the state laws in effect in 1860 and who had taken the amnesty oath would be entitled to vote or stand for election. The convention could then prescribe permanent voting and office-holding requirements, after which an election would be held for regular governors, state legislators, and members of Congress. The southern states had to proclaim the illegality of their ordinances of secession, repudiate all Confederate war debts, and ratify the Thirteenth Amendment, which prohibited slavery. The President would then revoke martial law, withdraw the federal troops, and recognize the state governments as reconstructed.

Except in Texas, within a few months the state conventions had finished their business, the state elections had been held, Presidential proclamations had retired the provisional governors, and Johnson had recognized the states as loyal. From the convening of Congress in December 1865 to Johnson's impeachment trial in 1868, the Radicals and the Johnsonians were at odds. On both sides a major issue was the Afro-Americans and their place in America. Johnson sided with the Democrats who demanded that the South remain a white man's country. The Radical Republicans, who were a minority in Congress, stated that the government was one of all men and that the goal of reconstruction was to give Afro-Americans equality before the law. But the motives of the Radicals were mixed. Some were firm believers in Afro-American equality on the grounds of principle. The influential Thaddeus Stevens, who was later buried in an Afro-American cemetery at his own request, also felt, in common with many Radicals, vindictiveness toward the South and an interest in perpetuating the ascendance of the Republican Party, not only as a symbol of the Union but as the protector of northern business interest.

The Johnsonians accused the Radicals of not having a sincere interest in Afro-Americans and of having, rather, a desire to exploit them, for, by giving the southern Afro-American the ballot, the Radicals would be assured of a Republican Party in the South. Meanwhile, Johnson strengthened the position of the Radicals by vetoing two laws that moderate Republicans believed he should have signed. The first extended the life and increased the powers of the Freedmen's Bureau, which had been created in March 1865 to feed, clothe, house, and render medical care to the thousands of illiterate, diseased, starving, and sometimes shiftless ex-slaves. The second was the Civil Rights Act of 1866. Johnson vetoed them even though the moderate Republicans made it clear that these laws were minimum terms for their continued support of his administration. The Radicals and moderates united to pass both laws over the President's vetoes. A few days later Johnson made a speech referring to some members of Congress as an irresponsible group usurping the powers of government. These remarks together with the vetoes made the break between Johnson and Congress inevitable. The last straw came with his reaction to the Fourteenth Amendment, which among other things defined citizenship, restricted the powers of the state in their relations with their inhabitants, forbade a state to deprive any person of life, liberty, or property without due process of law, forbade a state to deny any person equal protection of the law, required reduction of a state's representation in Congress for denial of suffrage, and disqualified former officeholders who participated in the Civil War. Johnson denounced the Fourteenth Amendment and urged the southern states not to ratify it. Ten of the eleven Confederate states took Johnson's advice.

This conflict between the President and Congress set the tone for the Congressional elections of 1866. Johnson went on a speaking tour denouncing Congress as domineering and tyrannical and urged that several Radicals be hanged. In doing so he alienated voters. The Republicans charged that Johnson was a drunkard, a rake, and kept a harem in the White House; they claimed that he was implicated in the assassination of

Lincoln, that he was a traitor plotting to turn the government over to southern rebels and northern Copperheads. The outcome was an overwhelming victory for the anti-Johnson Republicans. They won every northern gubernatorial contest and gained more than two-thirds majorities in both houses of Congress. Now the Radicals no longer had to fear Johnson's veto power—they could override it.

Congress, on February 1, 1865, passed the Thirteenth Amendment. This Amendment, which was ratified by a sufficient number of the states to become a part of the Constitution in December 1865, confirmed Lincoln's Emancipation Proclamation and freed all slaves who had not been included in his Proclamation, some 800,000.

CONGRESSIONAL RECONSTRUCTION

On December 2, 1865, the Republican caucus met and adopted a reconstruction program claiming that: (a) the whole question of reconstruction was the exclusive business of Congress, (b) the steps taken by the President were to be regarded as only provisional, (c) each house of Congress should postpone consideration of the admission of members from southern states, and (d) a Joint Committee of Fifteen should be elected by the Senate and House to inquire into the condition of the former Confederate states. This program was adopted by Congress. The Joint Committee was formed on December 26, 1865, and after an extensive investigation determined that (a) ex-rebels and Confederates had won control of all the ex-Confederate states, (b) northern settlers in the South were being persecuted, (c) Afro-Americans were being reduced to slavery, (d) nearly all the southern states had passed legislation called Black Codes, which stripped Afro-Americans of their social, civil, political, and economic rights, and (e) rebellious Southerners were not reconciled to defeat.

On March 2, 1867, Congress passed an act outlining its plan of political reconstruction. Three additional acts, which cleared up points left vague by the first, provided machinery for implementing the program and established safeguards against Presidential interference. Johnson vetoed these measures but Congress passed them over his vetoes. These acts repudiated the Johnson governments and divided the South into five military districts. The district commanders were required to enroll the qualified voters, including Afro-Americans but excluding those barred by the Fourteenth Amendment, and to hold elections for delegates to state constitutional conventions. Each convention was to frame a constitution providing for black as well as white male suffrage. When the constitution was ratified by popular vote the governor and state legislators could be elected. At the first meeting of the state legislature the Fourteenth Amendment had to be ratified. After Congress had approved the new state constitution and the Fourteenth Amendment had become a part of the United States Constitution, the state would be entitled to representation in Congress.

The Fourteenth Amendment, passed by Congress in June 1866 and ratified by the states in July 1868 in sufficient numbers to become a part of the Constitution, resulted from the rejection of Southern doctrines of state sovereignty and secession and also from the widespread doubt as to the constitutionality of the Civil Rights Act of 1866. This Amendment extended citizenship to Afro-Americans and thus nullified the infamous Dred Scott decision of 1857.

By 1868, six of the southern states had completed the process of reconstruction. Four delayed until after the Fourteenth Amendment had been ratified, and they were required to ratify the Fifteenth Amendment as well. By 1870 political reconstruction had been completed in all of the southern states.

The Fifteenth Amendment was a must for the Radical Republicans, for in providing for Afro-American suffrage in the ex-Confederate states they could not answer the question of why the suffrage was not a privilege to be exercised elsewhere in the nation. The Radicals did not want to resist the movement for national Afro-American suffrage for it suited their strategy—the enshrinement of Afro-American suffrage in the Constitution so that it could serve as the basis of Republican strength in the South. Accordingly, Congress passed the Fifteenth Amendment in February 1869, and it was ratified by a sufficient number of states to become a part of the Constitution in March 1870. It provided that the right to vote shall not be denied because of race, color, or previous condition of servitude.

In the face of rebukes by the electorate and Congress, Johnson doubled his efforts to sabotage Congressional reconstruction. He removed generals who were Radical sympathizers from their posts in the South, he fired the Secretary of War, who was also a supporter of the Radicals, and he refused to bring Jefferson Davis, the President of the Confederacy, to trial. To put a stop to Johnson's interference, impeachment proceedings were brought against him. After an extensive trial, the vote was 35 for guilty and 19 for not guilty. Inasmuch as the Constitution required a two-thirds vote by the Senate in impeachment cases, Johnson was saved by one vote. The Presidency had barely missed being taken over completely by the Congress.

THE DEMOCRATIC SOUTH

Each of the eleven ex-rebellious states during all or part of the decade between 1867 and 1877 fell under the control of the Radical Republicans. The ruling group consisted of (a) carpetbaggers (northern settlers in the South who actively supported the Radical Republicans), (b) scalawags (white southerners who collaborated with the Radical Republicans), and (c) Afro-Americans who constituted a majority in this coalition but whose influence was not as great as their numbers. At no time was there "black rule" in the South.

At the beginning of reconstruction, about 700,000 Afro-Americans and 660,000 whites were qualified as voters in the South. Of the whites of voting age, an estimated 150,000 were disfranchised or disqualified from holding office. Afro-Americans in South Carolina constituted about 60 percent of the population; in Mississippi, 55 percent; in Louisiana, 50 percent; in Florida, 47 percent; in Alabama, 46 percent; in Georgia, 44 percent; in Virginia, 41 percent; in North Carolina, 37 percent; in Arkansas, 26 percent; in Tennessee, 26 percent; and in Texas, 30 percent.

The first step in the organization of new southern state governments was the election of delegates to conventions to frame new state constitutions. In only two state conventions did Afro-Americans constitute 50 percent or more of the total number of delegates. The number of Afro-American and white delegates to state constitutional conventions under the Reconstruction Act of 1867 was:

State	No. of Blacks	No. of Whites	% of Blacks
Alabama	18	90	17
Arkansas	8	58	13
Florida	18	27	40
Georgia	33	137	19
Louisiana	49	49	50
Mississippi	17	83	17
North Carolina	15	118	11
South Carolina	76	48	61
Texas	9	81	10
Virginia	25	80	24

At the time that the new constitutions were ratified, elections were held for state officers and legislators. Afro-Americans did not hold dominant positions in the state governments that were established, even in those states where they formed the majority of the electorate. In the states where the black population was largest, they composed about half of the representation in the lower houses, but in each case the Senate and most major state offices remained in the hands of the whites. In the other states Afro-American representation was proportionately less. In all states the judiciary remained almost entirely in the hands of whites. In three states Afro-Americans were elected to the position of Lieutenant Governor, and in Louisiana the Lieutenant Governor served as acting governor during an interim period of forty-three days. White carpetbaggers and scalawags dominated the higher offices of the southern radical governments. Afro-Americans, although filling many city and county offices, ordinarily were unable to advance beyond the state legislatures, though they were able in some states to wield considerable influence. A number of black legislators gained the respect of many whites by ably championing various legislative innovations and reforms. Among the delegates sent to the United States Congress there were few Afro-Americans. By 1896 twenty had been elected to the House of Representatives and two to the Senate. Two congressmen from South Carolina each served five consecutive terms.

The charge that all Afro-American officeholders were illiterate and without integrity cannot stand. Some were college graduates and others had secondary education. Some were ex-slaves and others were freeborn. Among them were lawyers, preachers, farmers, public officials, and skilled craftsmen. Most were able to discharge their duties as public officials with competence and some with distinction. Among the Afro-American politicians who served ably during the Reconstruction Era were John M. Langston, John R. Lynch, H. R. Revels, B. K. Bruce, Joseph H. Rainey, James T. Rapier, and P. B. S. Pinchback. In addition, Afro-Americans served as state supreme court justices, justices of the peace, and superintendents of education.

Because of their political inexperience and economic helplessness, the Afro-American electorate was sometimes misled and victimized not only by southern white Democrats but also by the Republicans. However, it would be untrue to say that their political behavior was altogether passive or irresponsible. Suffrage was something Afro-American leaders had demanded for a number of years. Moreover, most Afro-Americans fully appreciated the importance of the ballot and took advantage of it with eagerness. As long as southern Democrats opposed Afro-American suffrage, the majority of Afro-American voters would continue to support the Republican Party. It was this that made it easy for the Union League and Freedmen's Bureau to mobilize and control the Afro-American vote.

All of the radical governments suffered from the inexperience, incompetence, and dishonesty of some officeholders. There was corruption, graft, and waste, just as there was in northern states and even in Congress. However, the southern legislatures wrote a large body of constructive provisions such as those providing for universal manhood suffrage, equality of civil rights, integrated public school systems, women's rights, systems of relief for the aged, and more-democratic tax systems. Other important measures abolished the Black Codes, Jim Crow practices, imprisonment for debt, and the use of whipping posts, stocks, and other barbarous types of punishment.

POLITICAL RECONSTRUCTION UNDONE

From the outset of the Reconstruction Era, conservatives of the South set out to destroy the radical coalition between Afro-Americans and whites. Initially they tried to convince ex-slaves that in reality the conservatives were the blacks' best friends, that the poor whites were their enemies, and that the carpetbaggers were foreign intruders who only wanted to exploit them. Afro-Americans, however, were not convinced. They helped build and intended to continue supporting the Republican Party. Oral persuasion failing, the conservatives resorted to violence. Groups were organized whose primary purpose was to prevent Afro-Americans and their white allies from exercising their political rights and to counter the Union League. The Ku Klux Klan, Knights of the White Camellia, Knights of the White Rose, Pale Faces, Red Jacks, Knights of the Black Cross, White Brotherhood, and Constitutional Guards were some of the secret terrorist groups who infested the South, committing atrocities against black people and their white allies.

To maintain the Afro-Americans' right to vote and to insure Republican control in the South, Congress proposed the Fifteenth Amendment, which became effective in March 1870; the Enforcement Acts of May 1870 and February 1871; and a law enacted in April 1871 that gave the President power to take direct action against terrorists who were preventing the exercise of civil and political rights of others.

For the most part these laws were ineffective: Evidence indicated that (a) efforts of the President to suppress the terrorists were inadequate—the local militia, which never had backing from the national government, was much too weak to be a decisive force, and furthermore all Afro-American federal troops had been withdrawn from the South by 1870; (b) passage in May 1872 of a general amnesty act reduced the number of former Confederate leaders barred from voting and holding office (indicating a new mood of conciliation in the Republican ranks); and (c) a serious split developed in the Republican Party because of the question of reconstruction.

The crisis came in the 1872 election. The Liberal Republicans adopted a platform that demanded the immediate and absolute removal of all disabilities imposed on account of the Civil War. The regular Republicans, with the Radicals still in control, adopted a platform endorsing the general course of the Grant administration. The Democratic Party, grasping the opportunity presented by the split in the Republican Party, endorsed the platform of the Liberal Republicans and chose as its candidate Horace Greeley, onetime abolitionist. The Afro-American vote went solidly behind the Republican ticket, and Grant won the election.

The Grant administration continued half-heartedly to support the radical cause in the South. In each state there was violence, and in 1875 Mississippi came close to having its own civil war. Thousands of blacks and even some whites were killed during the Reconstruction Era. On March 1, 1875, Congress passed the Civil Rights Act, which was designed to rectify a situation created largely by the determination of the South to re-create white supremacy.

The end came with the Presidential election of 1876. Tilden, the Democratic candidate, received a majority of the popular votes cast but only 184 of the 185 electoral votes necessary for election. Hayes, the Republican candidate, had 165, but 20 electoral college votes, mostly from three unredeemed southern states, were disputed. There seemed a possibility of a return to civil war, but a spirit of compromise prevailed. Northern supporters of Hayes held informal talks with Southerners very much like themselves—conservative businessmen. These Southerners were promised liberal appropriations for internal improvements in the South, a subsidy for a key railroad, a cabinet post and accompanying patronage, and the withdrawal of the last federal troops from the South. Key southern Democrats yielded to these offers, for they were hungry for northern capital and determined to control the governments of the southern states. Hayes was at last declared elected. The year 1877 thus saw the end of Reconstruction by means of a compromise that took the form of a stolen election. The Afro-American was simply abandoned in the shuffle of politics, profits, and sectional reconciliation.

Despite the conditions and the events, Afro-Americans fought desperately to keep their right to vote but met with only limited success. During this period they served in the assemblies and senates of all southern state legislatures, and there were many Afro-Americans holding offices in southern communities and a few in the United States Congress.

REFERENCES

Abbott, Martin, "Free Land, Free Labor, and the Freedmen's Bureau," *Agricultural History*, XXX (October 1956).

_____, "The Freedmen's Bureau and Negro Schooling in South Carolina," *South Carolina Historical Magazine*, LVII (April 1956).

Alderson, William T., Jr., "The Freedmen's Bureau and Negro Education in Virginia," *North Carolina Historical Review*, XXIX (January 1952).

Beale, Howard K., "On Rewriting Reconstruction History," *American Historical Review*, XLV (July 1940).

Benedict, Michael Lee, *The Impeachment and Trial of Andrew Johnson* (New York: The Norton Essays in American History, 1973).

Bentley, George R., *A History of the Freedmen's Bureau* (Philadelphia: University of Pennsylvania, 1955).

Blassingame, John W., *Black New Orleans, 1860-1880* (Chicago: The University of Chicago Press, 1973).

Boyd, Willis D., "Negro Colonization in the Reconstruction Era, 1865-1870," *Georgia Historical Quarterly* (December 1956).

Brown, Ira V., "Lyman Abbott and Freedman's Aid, 1865-1869," *Journal of Southern History*, XV (February 1949).

Cox, LaWanda, "The Promise of Land for the Freedman," *Mississippi Valley Historical Review*, XLV (December 1958).

_____, and John Cox, *Politics, Principle, and Prejudice, 1865-1866* (New York: Free Press of Glencoe, 1963).

Curry, Richard O., *Radicalism, Racism and Party Realignment: The Border States During Reconstruction* (Baltimore: The John Hopkins Press, 1969).

DeSantis, Vincent P., *Republicans Face the Southern Question* (Baltimore, Md.: Johns Hopkins Press, 1959).

Donald, Henderson H., *The Negro Freedman; Life Conditions of the American Negro in the Early Years After Emancipation* (New York: H. Schuman, 1952).

Drake, Richard B., "Freedmen's Aid Societies and Sectional Compromise," *Journal of Southern History*, XXIX (May 1963).

*Du Bois, W. E. B., *Black Reconstruction in America* (New York: Harcourt, Brace & Co., 1935 [World Publishing Co.]).

Durden, Robert F., *James Shepherd Pike: Republicanism and the American Negro, 1850-1882* (Durham, N.C.: Duke University Press, 1957).

————, *The Gray and the Black* (Baton Rouge: Louisiana State University Press, 1972).

Eaton, John, *Grant, Lincoln and the Freedmen* (New York: Longmans, Green & Co., 1907).

*Fleming, Walter L., ed., *Documentary History of Reconstruction, Political Military, Social Religious, Educational, and Industrial, 1865 to the Present Time* (Cleveland, Ohio: The A. H. Clark Co., 1906-1907 [McGraw-Hill]).

*Franklin, John H., *Reconstruction After the Civil War* (Chicago: The University of Chicago Press, 1961 [The University of Chicago Press]).

————, "Whither Reconstruction Historiography?" *Journal of Negro Education*, XVII, No. 4 (1948).

Harlan, Louis R., "Desegregation in New Orleans Public Schools During Reconstruction," *American Historical Review*, LXVII (April 1962).

Jackson, Luther P., *Negro Office-Holders in Virginia* (Petersburg, Va.: The Author, Virginia State College, 1945).

Johannsen, Robert W., ed., *Reconstruction 1865-1877* (New York: The Free Press, 1970).

Jones, Robert H., *Disrupted Decades: The Civil War and Reconstruction Years* (New York: Charles Scribner's and Sons, 1973).

Kelly, Alfred H., "The Congressional Controversy Over School Segregation, 1865-1875," *American Historical Review*, LXIV (April 1959).

Kendrick, Benjamin B., *The Journal of the Joint Committee of Fifteen on Reconstruction* (New York: Columbia University Press, 1914).

Lawson, Peggy, *The Glorious Failure: Black Congressman Robert Brown Elliott and Reconstruction in South Carolina* (New York: Norton, 1973).

Lester, John C., *The Ku Klux Klan: Its Origin, Growth, and Disbandment* (New York: The Neale Publishing Co., 1905).

*Lewinson, Paul, *Race, Class, and Party: A History of Negro Suffrage and White Politics in the South* (New York: Oxford University Press, 1936 [Grosset & Dunlap]).

Lynch, John R., *The Facts of Reconstruction* (New York: The Neale Publishing Co., 1913).

Mabry, William A., *Studies in the Disfranchisement of the Negro in the South* (Durham, N.C.: Duke University Press, 1938).

*McKitrick, Eric L., *Andrew Johnson and Reconstruction* (Chicago: The University of Chicago Press, 1960 [Phoenix, The University of Chicago Press]).

*McPherson, James M., *The Struggle for Equality: Abolitionists and the Negro in the Civil War and Reconstruction* (Princeton, N.J.: Princeton University Press, 1964 [Princeton University Press]).

Pierce, Paul S., *The Freedmen's Bureau, A Chapter in the History of Reconstruction* (New York: Haskell, 1904).

Quarles, Benjamin, *Black Abolitionists* (New York: Oxford Press, 1969).

Richardson, Joe M., *The Negro in the Reconstruction of Florida, 1865–1877* (Tallahassee, Fla.: Florida State University, 1965).

Riddleberger, Patrick W., "The Radical's Abandonment of the Negro During Reconstruction," *Journal of Negro History*, XLV (April 1960).

*Rose, Willie Lee, *Rehearsal for Reconstruction: The Port Royal Experiment* (Indianapolis: Bobbs-Merrill Co., 1964 [Vintage, Random House]).

Scheiner, Seth M., ed., *Reconstruction: A Tragic Era* (New York: Holt, Rinehart and Winston, 1968).

Singletary, Otis, *Negro Militia and Reconstruction* (Austin, Tex.: University of Texas Press, 1957).

Smith, Samuel D., *The Negro in Congress, 1870-1901* (Port Washington, N.Y.: Kennikat Press, 1940).

Stampp, Kenneth M., *Reconstruction: An Anthology of Revisionist Writings* (Baton Rouge: Louisiana State University Press, 1969).

———, *The Era of Reconstruction* (New York: Alfred A. Knopf, 1965 [Vintage, Random House]).

Taylor, Alrutheus A., *The Negro in the Reconstruction of Virginia* (Washington, D.C.: Association for the Study of Negro Life & History, 1926).

———, *The Negro in South Carolina During Reconstruction* (Washington, D.C.: Association for the Study of Negro Life & History, 1924).

———, *The Negro in Tennessee* (Washington, D.C.: Associated Publishers, Inc., 1941).

*Tindall, George B., *South Carolina Negroes, 1877-1900* (Columbia, S.C.: University of South Carolina Press, 1952 [Louisiana State University Press]).

Weisberger, Bernard, "The Dark and Bloody Ground of Reconstruction Historiography," *Journal of Southern History*, XXV (November 1959).

*Wharton, Vernon L., *The Negro in Mississippi, 1865-1890* (Chapel Hill, N.C.: University of North Carolina Press, 1947 [Harper & Row]).

Williamson, Joel, *After Slavery: The Negro in South Carolina During Reconstruction, 1861-1877* (Chapel Hill, N.C.: University of North Carolina Press, 1965).

Wood, Forrest G., *Black Scare: The Racist Response to Emancipation and Reconstruction* (Berkeley: University of California Press, 1968).

———, "On Revising Reconstruction History: Negro Suffrage, White Disfranchisement, and Common Sense," *Journal of Negro History,* LI (April 1966).

*Woodward, C. Vann, *Origins of the New South, 1877-1913* (Baton Rouge, La.: Louisiana State University Press, 1951 [Louisiana State University Press]).

18
Early Trade Unionism and the Afro-American

At most of the pre-Civil War Afro-American conventions, the question of improving the economic conditions of workers was discussed. However, a united movement for an Afro-American labor organization did not get under way until after the Civil War.

THE COLORED NATIONAL LABOR UNION

The first national expression of the Afro-American trade union movement was the convention held in 1869 in Washington, D.C. This convention, preceded by state gatherings, was called by the Maryland State Convention of Negro Workers. The convention bore many of the features of the Negro Convention Movement, but it was different in that stress was placed on trade unionism. The convention established the Colored National Labor Union and the delegates voted to affiliate with the National Labor Union, which had been founded in 1866 by white trade unionists who spoke out on the necessity of black-white labor solidarity but who had failed to organize Afro-American workers or recruit them into the National Labor Union. The convention also (a) placed heavy stress upon the question of getting land, (b) proposed the organization of integrated trade unions, (c) supported the establishment of cooperatives and women's suffrage, (d) condemned attempts to revive the American Colonization Society, and (e) supported the Republican Party.

Following the convention of 1869, a vigorous campaign was initiated to realize the objectives of the organization. However, in the struggle over southern reconstruction, the CNLU lost most of the trade union aspects of its program and became an appendage of the Republican Party. By 1874 it had perished.

Why wasn't there a closer working unity between the NLU and the CNLU? White unions failed to combat the employers' Jim Crow practices and policies in industry; white trade unionists barred Afro-Americans from the skilled trades; white trade unions failed to actively support the demands of Afro-Americans—land, suffrage, and equal rights; and white trade unionists insisted that Afro-Americans break their connection with the Republican Party and join the Labor Reform Party.

THE KNIGHTS OF LABOR

The National Labor Union was succeeded by the Knights of Labor. Like the NLU, the Knights of Labor aimed at uniting all workers without regard to race. The Knights organized blacks very actively but never adopted a policy of implementing their right to work in all industries and crafts; nor did it have a constructive program for the Klan-terrorized South. Nevertheless, it welcomed Afro-Americans, many of whom held official posts.

The policy of the Knights of Labor was to organize Afro-Americans and whites, either in single unions or separately, as the local workers decided. There were few mixed locals, however, for most white locals excluded Afro-Americans. Despite this white chauvinist attitude, the Knights of Labor represented the highest degree of Afro-American–white unity yet achieved. The organization began to decline after 1886, and by 1895 it was no longer a strong labor organization.

THE AMERICAN FEDERATION OF LABOR

The American Federation of Labor was formed in 1881. It was based upon craft unionism, as opposed to the mass-based organization of the NLU and the Knights of Labor. The appearance of the AF of L greatly hindered the organization of the Afro-American worker. The NLU and the Knights of

Labor had taken the position that Afro-American workers had to be organized. But the AF of L cultivated the interests of individual skilled or semi-skilled crafts and ignored and even worked against organization of black workers. The unions of skilled workers opposed Afro-Americans entering or working in the crafts; hence they barred Afro-Americans in practice, or by constitutional provisions, from joining the unions. This was the policy of many pioneer trade unions such as the Sons of Vulcan, Typographical Union, Railroad Brotherhoods, Bricklayers, and Carpenters. Some of the local craft unions deliberately admitted Afro-Americans, however, in order to control their access to jobs.

By refusing Afro-Americans access to skilled jobs in industry and to membership in the unions, the AF of L drove a wedge between the labor movement and Afro-Americans and tended to force them to the conclusion that if they wanted skilled work or any work, their only way to get it was by acting as strike-breakers.

REFERENCES

Bloch, Herman, "Labor and the Negro, 1866-1910," *Journal of Negro History*, L (July 1965).

Foner, Phillip S., *History of the Labor Movement in the United States*, 4 vols. (New York: International Publishers, Inc., 1947-1965).

_____, *Organized Labor and the Black Worker* (New York: Praeger Publishers, 1974).

Greene, Lorenzo J., and Carter G. Woodson, *The Negro Wage-Earner* (Washington, D.C.: Association for the Study of Negro Life & History, 1930).

Grob, Gerald N., "Organized Labor and the Negro Worker, 1865-1900," *Labor History*, I (Spring 1960).

Harris, Abram L., *The Negro as Capitalist: A Study of Bankruptcy and Business Among American Negroes* (Philadelphia: American Academy of Politics & Social Sciences, 1936).

Hill, Herbert, "In the Age of Gompers and After Racial Practices of Organized Labor," *New Politics*, IV (Spring 1965).

Kessler, Sidney, "The Organization of Negroes in the Knights of Labor," *Journal of Negro History*, XXXVII (July 1952).

Mandel, Bernard, "Samuel Gompers and the Negro Workers, 1886-1914," *Journal of Negro History*, XL (January 1955).

Matison, Sumner C., "The Labor Movement and the Negro During Reconstruction," *Journal of Negro History*, XXXIII (1948).

Northrup, Herbert R., *Organized Labor and the Negro* (New York: Harper & Brothers, 1944).

*Spero, Sterling D., and Abram L. Harris, *The Black Worker: The Negro and the Labor Movement* (New York: Columbia University Press, 1931 [Kennikat Press]).

Todes, Charlotte, *William H. Sylvis and the National Labor Union* (New York: International Publishers, Inc., 1942).

Wesley, C. H., *Negro Labor in the United States, 1850–1925, a Study in American Economic History* (New York: Vanguard Press, 1927).

19
Third Party Movements and the Afro-American

After the Civil War, agriculture was still the occupation of the majority of people in the South, blacks and whites. Besides the more than 250,000 Afro-Americans free before hostilities began and the 4,000,000 Afro-Americans freed by the war, there were about 8,000,000 whites who were principally farmers, with the small white farmer being the most numerous. Many blacks wanted to become landowners, but only a small minority achieved this goal. The bulk became sharecroppers and farm laborers.

The small white farmers hated the Afro-Americans because they feared them as competitors and they resented any rise in the social and political stature of Afro-Americans. As political reconstruction neared an end, the farmers in the South and West, both black and white, were beset with difficulties that defied solution. Inefficient farming methods, high interest charges, heavy debts, large-planter domination, tense race relations, and the lack of organization all worked to keep production costs high and farm income low. In this chaotic situation various associations sought to cope with these ailments.

THE COLORED NATIONAL FARMERS' ALLIANCE

Up to the mid-1880s, efforts aimed at improving the lot of the southern farmer were largely unsuccessful. Finally there emerged the Farmers' Alliance, a new organization that achieved an unprecedented measure of success. It was actually composed of three separate organizations—the Northern Alliance, the Southern Alliance, and the Colored National Farmers' Alliance.

The Southern Alliance was the strongest segment of the entire alliance movement. It arose out of the struggle of the farmers against large syndicates, monopolists, high freight and interest rates, and cattle kings. There were branches all over the South. In 1891 it was reported to have 35,000 lecturers and several million members. It admitted to membership small farmers, laborers, mechanics, schoolteachers, country doctors, and preachers. It especially excluded bankers, railroad officials, lawyers, large landowners, and merchants. Its constitution restricted membership to whites.

By 1890, the smaller Northern Alliance counted up to a million members. The Northern Alliance maintained an open organization and freely admitted Afro-Americans to membership, but there were few Afro-American farmers in the North.

Southern Alliance leaders realized that they could accomplish nothing politically without the support of Afro-Americans. The alliance that the white small farmers had refused to make during the antebellum years, the Civil War, and the Reconstruction Era was now unavoidable because of the desperate situation of both blacks and whites. However, rather than open its own doors to Afro-Americans, the white Southern Alliance leaders favored a separate organization of Afro-American farmers and farm workers, one which, nevertheless, they could control.

With the aid of the Southern Alliance, the Colored National Farmers' Alliance and Cooperative Union was launched in December 1886. In 1888 the national association was formed. Afro-Americans poured into the Alliance, and by 1891 it claimed 1,250,000 members in its twelve state organizations. Unwanted by the Democratic Party, sold out by the Republican Party, ostracized by the labor unions, and cast aside by other third-party organizations, where else could the Afro-American turn? Historians who have pictured the CNFA as a tool of the Southern Alliance are wrong, even though its founder and first superintendent was white. The CNFA possessed much of the militancy of the Union League and the Freedmen's Bureau. That the CNFA was not a mere appendage of the Southern Alliance is seen in the difference between the two groups over the Forced Bills and the cotton-pickers' strike called by the CNFA for a wage increase in 1891.

Although the Southern Alliance did not develop a specific program for Afro-Americans, in practice it was a force in defense of their rights. Out of necessity, many of its leaders, although white chauvinist in their outlook, had to express some spirit of cooperation. The very nature of its policy to win demands through political action involved the defense of the Afro-American's right to vote. The Southern Alliance also denounced lynchings and the convict-lease system, and generally defended the political rights of Afro-Americans. In both the North and the South, the CNFA was effective in electing white alliance members to city, county, state, and national offices. Then came the volte-face. After firmly gaining control in the South, those who previously advocated cooperation between the Southern Alliance and the CNFA now preached white supremacy. However, the organization began to deteriorate with the rise of the Populist Party, and by 1910 it had faded from the scene.

THE POPULIST MOVEMENT

Fresh from political victories in November 1890, the Southern Alliance met at Ocala, Florida, in December 1890. Delegates came from all over the South as well as from several northern and far western states, thus indicating the inroads the Southern Alliance had made in the North and West. After adopting a typical agrarian platform, the formation of a third party for political purposes was discussed. Midwestern delegates advanced arguments in behalf of a third party, while the majority of Southerners raised strong objections, finding it impossible to separate themselves from the Democratic Party that was firmly committed to maintaining white supremacy. The Southern Alliance deferred action on the issue until February 1892. Meanwhile, the Colored National Farmers' Alliance, meeting as a separate body, endorsed the move to form a third party.

The new-party advocates were impatient and assembled in May 1891. The majority of delegates came from the Midwest. The few southern delegates in attendance felt that the Democratic Party should be used as the political vehicle to secure the demands of the third party. This gathering confirmed the fears of the Southerners because Afro-American participation in the third party was welcomed on an equal basis. A third party convention was scheduled to assemble in February 1892, at which time social reformers united with farmers from the Midwest and wage-earners from the North, East, and Midwest, to form the People's or Populist Party.

The Populists believed that both races would support the Party: They knew that southern whites would never support the Republican Party and southern blacks would never support the Democratic Party. If both were educated along the same lines and were shown that their poverty and distress came from the same sources, the Populists' ranks would swell. But the role the Populists assigned to the Afro-American frightened many southern whites, and they decided to remain in the Democratic Party. They saw merit in most of the goals of the third party, but racial collaboration was simply too much.

The enthusiasm of Afro-Americans for the Populist Party varied. They supported the general principles of the third party regarding social reform, and in view of the position of the Democratic and Republican Parties on racial problems they had no better choice. Although the Populist Party had no specific program regarding Afro-Americans, it did propose reforms that would be beneficial to Afro-Americans and whites, to be accomplished by political means. Thus, while the association between the Southern Alliance and the CNFA was becoming estranged, there was close cooperation between Afro-Americans and the Populist Party. Afro-Americans were accepted as delegates and even as minor officers in the Party.

In the national election of 1892 and the congressional elections of 1894, the Populist Party showed its strength. It polled over one million votes and elected a considerable number of candidates to office. After 1896, however, the strength of the Party dropped rapidly because national prosperity was returning, the major parties took over some of the Party's program, and the Populists in some states had allied themselves with one of the major parties. The Populists could have swept the South if they had been able to rally and hold the votes of Afro-Americans. But they could not.

The tragic lesson to be learned from Populist history is that, as long as the Afro-American was a potential factor in politics, economic issues were subordinated to the racial problem in the South. Southerners wanted reform and relief but they wanted it through a vehicle that would not jeopardize white supremacy.

THE SOCIALIST PARTY

During the formative decades of Marxism in the United States, from the early 1850s onward, Marxists took little interest in the welfare of the Afro-American people. They advocated abolition of slavery and the slave trade, fought against the Confederacy, and after the Civil War agitated for bringing Afro-Americans into the trade union movement—but their efforts were half-hearted. Basically the Socialist Labor Party was apathetic on the Afro-American question. The problem was that the SLP failed to recognize the Afro-American's plight as a special problem. They assumed that the Afro-Americans were wage-earners and therefore that their problems were those of the working class in general. As a result they ignored such problems as the Jim Crow system and lynching.

Disgruntled members of the SLP and the Social Democratic Party amalgamated and in 1901 established the Socialist Party. It worked out a program of demands, but it too failed to include in its program specific demands for aiding Afro-Americans. In this respect the theory that Afro-Americans were only a division of the working class still prevailed and consequently the general demands for the workers would also meet their needs. Three black delegates were present at the founding convention, and at their insistence a resolution concerning Afro-Americans was reluctantly adopted. This resolution expressed sympathy with Afro-Americans in their difficult situation but did not condemn Jim Crow or lynching. However, it did invite Afro-Americans to join the Party in order to participate in the worldwide movement for economic emancipation. This was the only resolution relating to the situation of Afro-Americans passed by any socialist group from 1901 through 1912. It was not until after World War I, with the appearance of the Communist Party, that the Socialist Party began to bestir itself on the Afro-American question, and then only feebly.

In 1920 the Socialist Party demanded that Congress enforce the Thirteenth, Fourteenth, and Fifteenth Amendments and that Afro-Americans be accorded full civil, political, economic, and educational rights. But as late as its 1932 convention the Socialist Party rejected a motion demanding full social equality for Afro-Americans. With a philosophy such as this, the Socialist Party could not and did not become the party of the Afro-American people.

REFERENCES

Allen, J. S., *The Negro Question in the United States* (New York: International Publishers, 1936).

Edmonds, Helen G., *The Negro and Fusion Politics in North Carolina, 1894-1901* (Chapel Hill, N.C.: University of North Carolina Press, 1951).

*Hicks, John D., *The Populist Revolt; A History of the Farmers Alliance and the People's Party* (Minneapolis: University of Minnesota Press, 1931 [University of Nebraska Press]).

*Hirshon, Stanley, *Farewell to the Bloody Shirt: Northern Republicans the Southern Negro, 1872-1893* (Bloomington, Ind.: University of Indiana Press, 1926 [Quadrangle]).

Howe, I., and L. Coser, *The American Communist Party, a Critical History, 1919-1952* (Boston: Beacon Press, 1957; New York: Praeger, 1962).

Kipnis, Ira, *The American Socialist Movement, 1897-1912* (New York: Columbia University Press, 1952).

*Logan, Raford, *The Negro in American Life and Thought: The Nadir: 1877-1901* (1963 [Published as *The Betrayal and the Negro, From Hayes to Wilson* by Collier, Macmillan, 1965]).

Mabry, William A., *The Negro in North Carolina Politics Since Reconstruction* (Durham, N.C.: Duke University Press, 1940).

Martin, Roscoe C., *The People's Party in Texas, A Study in Third Party Politics* (Austin: University of Texas Press, 1933).

Morton, Richard L., *The Negro in Virginia Politics, 1865-1902* (Charlottesville, Va.: University of Virginia Press, 1919).

Sheldon, William D., *Populism in the Old Dominion: Virginia Farm Politics, 1885-1900* (Princeton, N.J.: Princeton University Press, 1935).

Thomas, Tony, *Black Liberation and Socialism* (New York: Pathfinder Press, 1974).

Wardlaw, Ralph W., *Negro Suffrage in Georgia, 1867-1930* (Athens, Ga.: University of Georgia Press, 1932).

*Woodward, C. Vann, *Origins of the New South, 1877-1913* (Baton Rouge, La.: Louisiana State University Press, 1951 [Louisiana State University Press]).

*_____, *Tom Watson, Agrarian Rebel* (New York: Oxford University Press, 1963 [Oxford University Press]).

20
White Philanthropy—
Black Self-Help

WHITE PHILANTHROPY

Because of the minimal change in the economic and social status of Afro-Americans during the Reconstruction Era and as a consequence of an erosion of their political rights, Afro-Americans turned to education, a field that white Southerners were generally willing to tolerate, in an effort to improve their status. However, with the expiration of the Freedmen's Bureau's aid and the very limited help from religious institutions, the already economically weak Afro-American schools seemed on their way to doom.

At this time there appeared on the scene several wealthy northern whites who were interested in stimulating education for Afro-Americans in the South. This was an age of educational philanthropy in the United States, and Afro-Americans benefited from the millions of dollars that were donated. Because the northern white philanthropists showed little desire to upset "the southern way of life," financial aid to Afro-American education was welcomed. The results were rewarding. Between the Reconstruction period and World War I, a number of Afro-American educational institutions were established, among them Morehouse College and Tuskegee Institute. There was an increase in the number of black teachers as well as students at all levels of education. Afro-American institutions already in existence were put on a more stable basis.

BLACK SELF-HELP

In the face of northern white philanthropy, Afro-American educational institutions did much to support themselves. Singing groups toured the nation and Europe soliciting funds. Fairs, carnivals, fish fries, sweet-potato festivals, and other activities were held in order to raise funds. By these and various other devices, Afro-Americans also aided in the establishment and growth of their institutions.

Even though education did much to uplift the Afro-American, it was necessary for Afro-Americans to establish a separate social and cultural existence because most white (north and south) maintained their traditional aloofness. The churches, although sometimes handicapped by internal dissension, responded to the challenge. Afro-American churches promoted education, encouraged the formation of literary societies, established welfare agencies, and founded nurseries, kindergartens, gymnasiums, employment bureaus, and handicraft clubs.

Afro-American fraternal orders and benefit associations were founded and those already in existence experienced remarkable growth. Mutual benefit societies sprang up and insurance companies were established. These institutions, established by Afro-Americans with money from the black community to serve the black community, were the first of their kind and served as a training ground for, and an example of, self-help. Another manifestation of the Afro-American's struggle to become self-sufficient was the establishment of independent orphanages, homes for the aged, hospitals, sanitariums, and numerous charitable organizations.

Afro-American conventions, although not the size they were before the Civil War, were held across the nation. At these conventions, educational, religious, and economic problems were discussed. Because of the atmosphere of segregation and discrimination that pervaded the United States, Afro-Americans were intent on finding solutions to the problems that affected them.

As reflected in literature, blacks began to achieve intellectual independence. In biographies Afro-Americans told of their experiences. A new interest in the past was expressed by many publications on Negro history. Novels and short stories were published, and Afro-American newspapers and magazines experienced growth.

REFERENCES

Bond, Horace Mann, *The Education of the Negro in the American Social Order*, rev. ed. (New York: Octagon Books, 1966).

Bullock, Henry Allen, *A History of Negro Education in the South; From 1619 to the Present* (Cambridge, Mass.: Harvard University Press, 1967).

Du Bois, W. E. B., *The Negro in Business* (Atlanta, Ga.: Atlanta University, 1899).

*Harlan, Louis R., *Separate and Unequal: Public School Campaigns and Racism in the Southern States, 1901-1915* (Chapel Hill, N.C.: University of North Carolina Press, 1958 [Atheneum]).

Harris, A., *The Negro as Capitalist, a Study of Banking and Business Among American Negroes* (Philadelphia: American Academy of Politics and Social Sciences, 1936).

Holmes, Dwight Oliver W., *Evolution of the Negro College* (New York: Columbia University Press, 1934).

Range, Willard, *The Rise and Progress of Negro Colleges in Georgia, 1865-1949* (Athens, Ga.: University of Georgia Press, 1951).

Rubin, Louis D., *Teach the Freeman: The Correspondence of Rutherford B. Hayes and the Slater Fund for Negro Education* (Baton Rouge, La.: Louisiana State University Press, 1959).

Simmons, William J., *Men of Mark: Eminent, Progressive, and Rising (1887-1891)* (New York: Arno Press, 1968).

Thornbrough, Emma Lou, "The National Afro-American League, 1887-1908," *Journal of Southern History*, XXVII (November 1961).

Washington, Booker T., *The Negro in Business* (Boston: Hertel, Jenkins & Co., 1907).

Woodson, Carter G., *History of the Negro Church* (Washington, D.C.: Associated Publishers, Inc., 1921).

21
Booker T. Washington
vs. W.E.B. Du Bois

BOOKER T. WASHINGTON

As a youth Booker T. Washington attended Hampton Institute where he was taught early that physical labor promoted honesty, intelligence, and the acquisition of land and homes, and that the learning of a skilled trade was vital. When Washington arrived at Tuskegee, he believed southern whites had to be convinced that the education of Afro-Americans was in the best interest of the entire South. Hence he assured the community that the students were there to serve them. As the students began to provide the community with goods and services, the hostility of whites began to disappear, and Washington, noting the beneficial effects his program was having, came to believe that this was the best way to better the status of Afro-Americans. He soon became an advocate of vocational education, prescribing a program of training Afro-Americans to become farmers, skilled artisans, and domestic servants. He counseled blacks to remain in the South, to become economically self-sufficient, and to remain socially separate from whites. He did not deprecate the study of the liberal arts, but he regarded it as impractical. Washington did not attack Jim Crow or seek to promote the suffrage of Afro-American people; instead, he sought to conciliate whites.

Washington's doctrine of vocational education for the Afro-American was generally accepted by whites, north and south. Some northern whites saw in it a formula for peace among the races in the South; others, believing Afro-Americans inherently inferior, viewed the program as leading them to their proper place in society; others considered it a method of creating a great labor pool. Southern whites liked the program because it did not involve political, civil, and social aspirations and it would consign Afro-Americans to an inferior economic status.

Because Washington's program conciliated whites, substantial contributions were given to Tuskegee and other institutions that adopted the Washington philosophy. Washington's prestige grew to the point where he was regarded as the spokesman for the entire Afro-American community.

W. E. B. DU BOIS

A small group of Afro-American leaders were not satisfied with Washington's program and the techniques he proposed to use in raising the status of the Afro-American. The most outspoken was W. E. B. Du Bois. Educated at Fisk, Harvard, and Berlin, Du Bois was an instructor at Atlanta University where he was conducting a series of studies on the condition of Afro-Americans in the South at the same time Washington was developing his program of vocational education.

Generally, Du Bois opposed Washington's program, indicating that it was not broad enough in its scope and objectives and that the curriculum was too narrowly defined. He did not approve of the manner in which Washington ignored the Afro-American's civil and political inferiority, the violence being exacted on the Afro-American community, and the economic exploitation of the black masses. Du Bois admitted that Washington had become the spokesman for the Afro-American community, but he regarded this position as a result of white acclaim and not because of esteem by the black community. Du Bois and others who opposed Washington lost the support, financial and otherwise, of whites who could not understand why all Afro-Americans did not think like Washington.

THE SAME END

Both Washington and Du Bois wanted the same thing, first-class citizenship for the Afro-American, but their methods of achieving it differed. Because of the interest in the immediate goals of Washington's program, whites did not realize that he looked forward to the complete acceptance and integration of Afro-Americans in American life. He believed that Afro-Americans, starting with so little, would have to work up gradually and achieve positions of power and responsibility before they could demand equal citizenship. If this meant sacrifice or temporarily assuming a position of inferiority, so be it.

Du Bois fully understood Washington's program, but believed that although vocational education was fine, it was not the solution. Afro-Americans should study humanities as well as the arts and face the same problems and have the same rights as others similarly situated. Afro-Americans should not have to sacrifice their constitutional rights in order to achieve a status that was already guaranteed.

There were other black individuals and organizations who protested Booker T. Washington's educational, social, and political philosophy, including the National Association of Colored Men (founded by R. T. Greener in 1896) and the American Negro Academy (founded by Alexander Crumwell, Francis J. Grimke, and others in 1897). The Negro Industrial and Agricultural Association of Virginia and the Colored Men's Association of Alabama, in their efforts to prevent the enactment of laws which would disenfranchise southern blacks, were also critical of Washington. William Monroe Trotter, a Harvard graduate and publisher of the Boston *Guardian*, and T. Thomas, editor of the New York *Age*, also took Washington to task for his policies of accommodation.

REFERENCES

*Broderick, Francis L., *W. E. B. Du Bois: Negro Leader in a Time of Crisis* (Stanford, Calif.: Stanford University Press, 1959 [Stanford University Press]).

Du Bois, Shirley G., *His Day is Marching On: A Memoir of W. E. B. Du Bois* (New York: J. B. Lippincott, 1971).

*Du Bois, W. E. B., *The Souls of Black Folk: Essays and Sketches* (Chicago: A. C. McClurg & Co., 1901 [Fawcett World]).

Harlan, Louis R., "Booker T. Washington and the White Man's Burden," *The American Historical Review*, LXXI (January 1966).

_____, *Booker T. Washington: The Making of a Black Leader 1856-1901* (New York: Oxford University Press, 1972).

_____, *The Booker T. Washington Papers*, 3 vols. (Urbana: University of Illinois, 1972, 1974).

*Hawkins, Hugh, *Booker T. Washington and His Critics: Problem of Negro Leadership* (Boston: D. C. Heath and Company, 1962 [Heath, Raytheon]).

Kellogg, Charles F., *NAACP 1909-1920*, Vol. 1, (Baltimore: The Johns Hopkins Press, 1967).

Mathews, Basil Joseph, *Booker T. Washington, Educator and Interracial Interpreter* (Cambridge, Mass.: Harvard University Press, 1948).

*Meier, August, *Negro Thought in America, 1880-1915* (Ann Arbor, Mich.: University of Michigan Press, 1963 [University of Michigan Press]).

Morton, Robert Russa, *Finding a Way Out, An Autobiography* (New York: Doubleday & Company, 1920).

Rudwick, Elliot M., *W. E. B. Du Bois: A Study in Minority Group Leadership* (Philadelphia: University of Pennsylvania Press, 1960).

*Spencer, Samuel R., *Booker T. Washington and the Negro's Place in American Life* (Boston: Little, Brown & Co., 1955 [Little]).

Washington, Booker T., *The Negro in the South: His Economic Progress in Relation to His Moral and Religious Development* (London: T. Fisher Unwin, 1909).

*_____, *Up From Slavery* (New York: Doubleday & Co., 1933 [Dell]).

22
American Expansionism

AMERICA'S BLACK EMPIRE

American imperialism began to take definite shape after the middle of the nineteenth century. With the purchase of Alaska, the annexation of the Hawaiian Islands, and the acquisition of the Samoan and other Pacific Islands, the United States by 1900 had acquired an empire composed primarily of darker peoples. But it was in the Western Hemisphere that the United States, through the Monroe Doctrine and Dollar Diplomacy, pursued its imperialistic policy most vigorously. Through financial and political manipulations, millions of persons of mixed blood in the Western Hemisphere were brought under the influence and control of the United States.

At the end of the Spanish-American War, Spain relinquished its claim to sovereignty over Cuba and, in lieu of a war indemnity, ceded to the United States Puerto Rico and other insular possessions in the West Indies. When the United States acquired the Panama Canal Zone and the Virgin Islands, its domination of the Western Hemisphere was all but complete. Santo Domingo and Haiti, like other Latin-American nations, were secured by United States' policy of Dollar Diplomacy. Upon the payment of twenty million dollars by the United States at the end of the Spanish-American War, Spain relinquished the Philippines and thus gave the United States another foothold in the Pacific.

The interest of the United States in Africa stems from the early days of the founding of Liberia, when American business and industry began to intimately participate in, and thereby affect, the economic life of that country. From this time the United States, by employing aid to underdeveloped nations, manipulating import and export duties, and making enormous investments in African industries, has managed to wield substantial influence in the development and administration of domestic and international policy in several African nations. As a consequence the United States has brought under its influence, and in some cases under its actual control, millions of black people, thus becoming an imperialistic power like its European counterparts.

AFRO-AMERICANS AND THE SPANISH-AMERICAN WAR

Recession and rigid Spanish control had inspired numerous insurrections in Cuba around 1800. These incidents became more frequent and intense especially between 1865-1880 when Cubans showed their determination to have their independence by openly revolting. This drive for independence coincided with an increasing economic interest of the United States in Cuba due to substantial material investments in the island, and a humanitarian interest resulting from incidents of brutality committed by the Spanish.

In 1895 a general revolt was staged as Cubans launched their fight for independence. As a result of the widespread destruction of property and the loss of lives, in January 1898 the American battleship *Maine* was ordered to Havana to protect American lives and property. On February 15, 1898, an explosion sank the *Maine*, setting off a train of events that culminated in war shortly thereafter between the United States and Spain.

From the beginning of hostilities, Afro-Americans were involved. There were at least thirty on the *Maine*, but even prior to this Afro-Americans aided Cubans in their quest for independence. Therefore, when the President called for volunteers, Afro-Americans responded enthusiastically.

Under the first call for volunteers only the organized state militias were acceptable. This left out Afro-Americans almost completely because very few Afro-Americans were in the northern militias and the southern states barred them altogether. In northern communities Afro-Americans formed volunteer regiments and offered their services to the states, but under the law governing the National Guard they could not be accepted. Afro-Americans appealed to the President, but he referred the matter to the War Department where nothing was done. Under the pressure of Afro-American leaders, Congress passed a special bill authorizing the recruitment of ten Afro-American regiments, but only four regiments were raised since the need for servicemen had lessened and because individual states had begun to permit the enlistment and recruitment of blacks.

At the time there were four black regiments in the Regular Army that had been activated shortly after the close of the Civil War and had performed duties in the Indian wars in the West and in border service. As in previous wars, the question of Afro-American officers plagued the military and civilian leaders. Most white officers regarded Afro-Americans as unfit for leadership and pointed out that there was only one Afro-American commissioned officer in the Regular Army. Furthermore, the War Department had ordered that officers above the rank of second lieutenant in the specially created Afro-American regiments be white; however, under the pressure of Afro-American leaders, the President commissioned about one hundred Afro-American second lieutenants in the volunteer service.

In the action that brought victory to the United States, only the Afro-Americans in the four Regular Army regiments saw any appreciable amount of service. Afro-American troops that did see action fought courageously and won the praises of Americans and Cubans alike. The reaction of Teddy Roosevelt was varied, depending upon the occasion, even though it has been claimed that Afro-American regiments saved his Rough Riders from annihilation.

The service that Afro-Americans rendered in the Navy was relatively inconsequential. Discrimination was widespread. To be sure, Afro-Americans were on every ship used in the hostilities, but they were employed primarily in menial capacities: messmen and officers' orderlies. Even so, there were several instances of heroism.

On the home front, Afro-American troops were segregated and discriminated against. When Afro-American soldiers were in Tampa, Florida, awaiting shipment to Cuba, they were not allowed to go ashore unless a white officer led an entire company ashore. They were assigned to the holds of the ships where there was very little light or air; they were not permitted to mingle with white soldiers. As they passed through cities en route to ports of embarkation they were frequently stoned and spat upon by whites.

REFERENCES

Bailey, Thomas A., *Diplomatic History of the American People* (New York: F. S. Crofts & Co., 1942).

Glass, Edward L. N., *The History of the Tenth Cavalry, 1886-1901* (Tucson, Ariz.: Acme Printing Co., 1921).

Guthrie, James M., *Campfires of the Afro-American* (Philadelphia: Afro-American Publishing Co., 1899).

Johnson, Edward A., *History of Negro Soldiers in the Spanish-American War, and Other Items of Interest* (Raleigh, N.C.: Capital Printing Co., 1899).

Logan, R., *Diplomatic Relations of the U.S. with Haiti, 1776-1891* (Chapel Hill, N.C.: University of North Carolina Press, 1941).

Lynk, Miles V., *The Black Troopers; Or the Daring Heroism of the Negro Soldiers in the Spanish-American War* (Jackson, Tenn.: M.V. Lynk Publishing House, 1899).

*Millis, Walter, *The Martial Spirit* (New York: Houghton Mifflin, 1931 [Viking Press]).

*Pratt, Julius W., *The Expansionists of 1898* (Baltimore, Md.: Johns Hopkins Press, 1936 [Quadrangle]).

Weston, Rubin F., *Racism in U.S. Imperialism: The Influence of Racial Assumptions in American Foreign Policy 1893-1946* (Columbia: University of South Carolina Press, 1972).

*Williams, William A., *The Tragedy of American Diplomacy* (Cleveland, Ohio: World Publishing Co., 1959 [Dell]).

23
The Turn of the 20th Century

DISFRANCHISEMENT

After the Hayes sellout of 1877, Southerners set out to strip Afro-Americans of all their gains, especially of the right to vote. All over the South a campaign of white supremacy was carried on in an effort to alienate whites from Afro-Americans. The black-white cooperation during the Alliance and Populist movements of the 1880s and 1890s was precarious and handicapped from the start by suspicion and prejudice. By 1890 a majority of southern whites were convinced that propaganda of white supremacy and violence were not enough to nullify Afro-Americans as a political force and that the Afro-Americans had to be stripped of their right to vote by legislation. Meanwhile, the North had lost all interest in protecting Afro-American rights and was willing to permit disfranchisement in the interest of intersectional reconciliation.

Mississippi adopted a poll tax and a literacy test as requirements for voters in 1890, and by 1910 every southern state had adopted some type of disfranchising scheme. These provisions eliminated virtually all the Afro-Americans from the voting lists, nullifying the rights guaranteed by the Fourteenth and Fifteenth Amendments.

LIFE IN THE CITIES

After the turn of the twentieth century, Afro-Americans began to divorce themselves from the soil and move into urban centers in search of better economic opportunities. Coincident with this migration was the rise of the Afro-American community within the city. In time, Afro-Americans became a significant segment of the urban population of several northern cities and outnumbered whites in many southern cities.

As employment opportunities in the cities were few, Afro-Americans had great difficulty securing anything except the less attractive jobs. Even after the prospects of securing any employment were almost nil, Afro-Americans continued to flock to the cities, thereby jeopardizing the opportunities of those already there. As a consequence, black ghettos began to emerge, for white landlords were determined to segregate Afro-Americans in one section of the city; and many municipalities approved this practice by enacting ordinances that provided for segregated housing.

All of the social ills associated with ghetto life developed: poor health, high mortality rate, crime and juvenile delinquency, and family disorganization and disintegration.

VIOLENCE

Terrorism and violence continued unabated at the turn of the twentieth century. Between 1880 and 1900 there had been more than 2500 lynchings. In 1901 more than 100 Afro-Americans were lynched, and before the outbreak of World War I, the number rose to more than 1000. These dastardly acts occurred mostly in the South, but in several northern states race riots and lynchings occurred. Up to the outbreak of World War I, Afro-American men, women, and children were burned, shot, slashed to pieces, and dragged to death. The lynchings, carried out in the name of "justice," were usually committed with full knowledge and sometimes with the participation of the local authorities. The federal government did little to stop this wholesale slaughter.

PROGRAMS OF ACTION

On the eve of "the war to make the world safe for democracy," Afro-Americans suffered from the most acute forms of exploitation and terror.

They were shamelessly robbed as tenant farmers and sharecroppers, stripped of their right to vote, systematically insulted by Jim Crow, barred from industry, crowded into the filthy ghettos, and thrown into jails and onto chain gangs for the most trivial offenses. Above these abuses hung the menace of death. Out of this environment grew several organizations.

The Niagara Movement

In 1905 a group of Afro-Americans organized the Niagara Movement. Its "Declaration of Principles" was a resounding protest against the many outrages perpetrated against the black people of America, and it called on black people to fight against these injustices. It demanded the right to vote, full education, justice in court and service on juries, equal treatment in the armed forces, health facilities, abolition of Jim Crow, and the enforcement of the Thirteenth, Fourteenth, and Fifteenth Amendments. It protested vigorously against the unchristian attitude of religious institutions, and it denounced the discriminatory policies of employers and trade unions.

The formation of the Niagara Movement marked a turning point in the history of the Afro-American, for it constituted the beginning of a more militant policy of struggle against Jim Crow and terrorism.

The NAACP

The National Association for the Advancement of Colored People was organized in May 1909 by fifty-five Afro-Americans and white liberals. Absorbing many of the militant leaders of the Niagara Movement, the NAACP endorsed the philosophy of the Movement; however, its program was not as clear nor its organization as aggressive, largely due to the composition of its executive board. The Niagara Movement was an Afro-American organization with militant activists at the helm, whereas the NAACP was controlled by white liberals, Du Bois being the only Afro-American among the original executive officers.

The NAACP carried on vigorous campaigns against lynching and Jim Crow. It fought to secure the franchise and to put an end to segregation and discrimination. In the beginning most white philanthropists did not support the Niagara Movement and its successor, the NAACP. They preferred the less alarming activities of Booker T. Washington. Later on, however, the organization, by its increasingly conservative course, was able to win their support, and contributions poured in. The influence and participation of white philanthropists in the Afro-American organizations was both a handicap and a help in the Afro-American's struggle for equality.

The influence of whites served to tone down the radicalism of the black leadership, while money and legal assistance from whites helped the NAACP win important legal victories.

The Urban League

The Urban League, founded in 1911 as the National League on Urban Conditions Among Negroes, resulted from the merger of three social service agencies. The moderate quality of the League's program seems to have derived from its social welfare origins. The League thought the basic problem was to enable black migrants from the South to cope with urban life. As a predominantly social service organization, the League devoted itself to placing Afro-Americans in jobs and to the creation of better housing, school facilities, public playgrounds, health clinics, and similar institutions in black communities. Racism was not as yet conceived as an obstacle in the northern cities.

The Urban League had a composition similar to the NAACP, with white liberals in control. The League shunned politics and devoted itself to questions that related to the economic welfare of the Afro-American. Because of the League's conservative policies, from the outset it had philanthropic backing that, for a time at least, was withheld from the less conservative NAACP.

YMCA and YWCA

The first Afro-American YMCA was organized in 1853, but it was not until after the Civil War that the black YMCA became affiliated with the white YMCA movement. In the late 1880s several Afro-Americans were made salaried officers. Their duty was to give special attention to the problems of Afro-Americans in urban areas. Shortly after 1900, with the aid of white philanthropists several Afro-American branches of the YMCA were organized. There were relatively few black YWCAs prior to the turn of the twentieth century, and it was not until the outbreak of World War I that a strong movement developed to organize Afro-American women in the YWCA.

Other Efforts

There were other isolated efforts to solve the acute problems of the Afro-American. Settlement houses were established, neighborhood associations formed, and housing developments constructed in various communities in the North and South.

REFERENCES

Baker, Ray S., *Following the Color Line* (New York: Harper & Row, 1964).

Bontemps, Arna, and Jack Conroy, *Anyplace But Here* (New York: Hill & Wang, 1966 [Hill & Wang]).

Du Bois, W. E. B., *Dusk of Dawn* (New York: Harcourt, Brace & Co., 1940 [Schocken Books]).

———, *The Philadelphia Negro* (Philadelphia: Lease to House Survey [New York: Schocken Books, 1967]).

Harris, A. L., *The Black Worker: The Negro and the Labor Movement* (New York: Columbia University Press, 1931).

Hughes, Langston, *Fight for Freedom: The Story of the NAACP* (New York: W. W. Norton, 1962).

Jack, Robert L., *History of the National Association for the Advancement of Colored People* (Boston: Meador Publishing Co., 1943).

Kellogg, Charles Flint, *NAACP: A History of the National Association for the Advancement of Colored People, 1909-1920*, Vol I (Baltimore, Md.: Johns Hopkins Press, 1967).

Logan, Frenise A., *The Negro in North Carolina, 1876-1894* (Chapel Hill, N.C.: University of North Carolina Press, 1964).

Mooreland, J. E., "The Young Men's Christian Association Among Negroes," *Journal of Negro History*, IX (January 1924).

Parris, Guichard, and Lester Brooks, *Blacks in the City: A History of the National Urban League* (Boston: Little, Brown & Co., 1971).

Raper, A., *The Tragedy of Lynching* (Chapel Hill, N.C.: University of North Carolina Press, 1933).

Reuter, E. B., *The American Race Problem: A Study of the Negro* (New York: Thomas Y. Crowell Co., 1927).

*Rudwick, Elliot M., *Race Riot at East St. Louis, July 2, 1917* (Carbondale, Ill.: Southern Illinois University Press, 1964 [World Publishers]).

Shay, Frank, *Judge Lynch, His First Hundred Years* (New York: I. Washburn, Inc., 1938).

Stone, Alfred H., *Studies in the American Race Problem* (New York: Doubleday & Co., 1908).

Thirty Years of Lynching, 1889-1918, report by NAACP (New York: NAACP, 1919).

Tindall, George B., *The Emergence of the New South 1913-1945* (Baton Rouge, La.: Louisiana State University Press, 1967).

Weiss, Nancy J., *The National Urban League 1910-1940* (New York: Oxford University Press, 1974).

Wood, L. Hollingsworth, "The Urban League Movement," *Journal of Negro History*, IX (January 1924).

Woodson, Carter G., *A Century of Negro Migration* (Washington, D.C.: Association for the Study of Negro Life & History, 1918).

*Woodward, C. Vann, *The Strange Career of Jim Crow* (New York: Oxford University Press, 1955 [Oxford University Press]).

Wynes, Charles, *Race Relations in Virginia, 1870-1902* (Charlottesville, Va.: University of Virginia Press, 1961).

24
The Afro-American and World War I

INITIAL ATTITUDE

War was declared on April 6, 1917. Many Afro-Americans were not enthusiastic in their support of the war, especially a group of Afro-American socialists who stated that the war was being waged by imperialistic powers in order to obtain more foreign markets, more colonies, and more people to exploit. But once the United States entered the war, a split occurred among Afro-American socialists with the majority coming out in support of the war, especially after President Wilson's assurance that the war was being waged to make the world more democratic.

From the outset the black press endorsed the war, but *The Crisis*, publicity organ of the NAACP, took this opportunity to make certain demands on the federal government. It demanded that: (1) Afro-Americans be allowed to serve on the battlefield and to receive adequate training, (2) black troops be led by Afro-American officers who had been properly trained, (3) lynching be stopped, (4) the right to vote be insured, (5) universal and free public education be assured, (6) Jim Crow be abolished, and (7) equal civil rights be restored. *The Crisis* also urged blacks to "close ranks" with white Americans to defeat the nation's enemies. Needless to say, these demands were ignored.

AFRO-AMERICANS IN THE WAR

Approximately 2,291,000 Afro-Americans registered in the draft, and 367,000 were accepted. There were approximately 400,000 Afro-Americans in the Army and Navy. There was no place at all for Afro-Americans in the Army Air Forces and Coast Guard. Some 200,000 Afro-Americans were sent overseas. Black soldiers were segregated into Jim Crow regiments with white officers. Only after a bitter struggle was an Afro-American officers' training camp established; however, the graduates, some 1,400 of them, were ostracized by white officers and generally slandered as inefficient, corrupt, laxy, and immoral.

About three-fourths of the Afro-Americans who were sent overseas were relegated to work as day laborers in the Service of Supply. As cooks, orderlies, truck drivers, and stevedores they were subjected to every insult imaginable, both verbal and physical. But Afro-American troops who were given a chance to fight acquitted themselves with honor. Entire regiments, companies, squads, and individuals were cited for valor. The French, especially, praised Afro-American troops for their bravery.

Army officials were alarmed that the black troops would be attracted by the democratic way the French people treated them. Hence orders were issued commanding Afro-American troops not to associate with French women, prohibiting them from attending French dances, and otherwise instituting Jim Crow policies in France. A pamphlet entitled *Secret Information Concerning Black American Troops*, which set forth the grossest white supremacist slander, was issued warning the French not to associate with the degenerate, rapist Afro-American troops.

To add insult to injury, President Wilson sent a prominent Afro-American to France to warn black troops not to expect the democracy they had experienced in France when they returned to the United States, but that they must be content with the same status they had held before being sent abroad. Afro-American troops in the United States were "Jim Crow'd." The YMCA and similar organizations refused them board and lodging. They were refused rooms in hotels and denied entrance to restaurants. These abuses led to many clashes between whites and black troops, the most serious incident taking place in Houston, Texas, in August 1917. In retaliation for deadly assault upon two local Afro-Americans, black troops killed seventeen whites. For this thirteen Afro-American soldiers were hanged, forty-one sentenced to life in prison, and four given shorter terms.

In conjunction with the World War I peace conference and the establishment of the League of Nations, an international conference of black people was held in Paris. Fifty-seven delegates attended, including sixteen Afro-Americans, twenty West Indians, and twelve Africans. The conference adopted minimum demands for democratic treatment of black people in various parts of the world, but those nations who had just fought a war to make the world a better place for democracy ignored these demands. This Pan-African Conference emphasized the solidarity of black people throughout the world, and it set a precedent that was to be followed in future years.

NORTHWARD MIGRATION

During the course of World War I, southern Afro-Americans had migrated north to escape the conditions of oppression and exploitation and to fill the jobs created by the war. Employers encouraged this migration by sending labor recruiters into the South. It is estimated that between 1915 and 1918 approximately 500,000 Afro-Americans trekked north. An equal number was to follow during the twenties. Alarmed southern leaders intimidated northern labor recruiters and sometimes required them to pay prohibitive fees. Propaganda campaigns were inaugurated to induce Afro-Americans to remain in the South, and when this did not work terrorist methods were used.

Arriving in the North, Afro-Americans flocked into the industrial centers where they found jobs in the war industries. As always these jobs were the hardest and poorest paid, but at the same time they were better than any jobs that Afro-Americans had been able to get previously. Numerous attempts were made to get unions to recruit Afro-American workers. Labor conventions, generally, passed resolutions endorsing such efforts by Afro-Americans, but characteristically nothing came of them. Organized labor remained wedded to its traditional Jim Crow policy. Segregation placed a strain on labor relations between blacks and whites, especially when Afro-Americans were used as strikebreakers.

The migration to the North during World War I and the postwar years had many favorable consequences for the Afro-American. Most important, it greatly increased the size of the black middle class and intelligentsia; it stimulated Afro-American culture and mobilized the Afro-American press along with other black institutions; and it gave Afro-Americans a new militancy and a sense of dignity and power.

POSTWAR REACTION

Shortly after the war ended, industrialists opened an offensive against the trade unions to strip them of the gains they had won during the war. Strikes raged in many industries. Organized labor was fighting desperately against the open shop. Afro-Americans were caught in the middle—discriminated against by unions and used as strikebreakers by employers. Their dilemma was intensified by the economic crisis of 1920–1921, during which wages were cut and over five million laborers were unemployed.

During the same period the Ku Klux Klan grew to a membership of five million. The Klan was especially violent toward Afro-American veterans and tried to burn out any notions of social, civil, and political equality the veterans mights have acquired in France. In the South floggings, brandings, tarrings and featherings, hangings, and burnings were common. From 1915 to 1918, there were 199 Afro-Americans lynched. In the postwar years, 1919 to 1922, there were 239 more killed. These figures do not include the great number of unrecorded lynchings.

The reaction in the North was equally bad. Because of the failure to achieve adequate jobs, housing, schools, and recreational facilities, tension developed between Afro-Americans and whites. White hoodlums frequently provoked race riots in parts of the Northeast and Midwest. In the summer and fall of 1919, there were twenty-five race riots. The most violent one, in Chicago, lasted thirteen days: thirty-eight persons were killed, including fifteen whites and twenty-three Afro-Americans; over 500 were injured, including 178 whites and 342 Afro-Americans.

REFERENCES

Barbeau, Arthur E., and Floretta Henri, *The Unknown Soldiers: Black American Troops in World War I* (New York: Temple University Press, 1974).

Beer, George L., *African Questions at the Paris Peace Conference* (New York: The Macmillan Co., 1923).

Chicago Commission on Race Relations, *The Negro in Chicago: A Study of Race Relations and a Race Riot* (Chicago: University of Chicago Press, 1922).

Clarke, Kenneth B., "Morale of the Negro on the Home Front: World Wars I and II," *Journal of Negro Education*, XII (Summer 1943).

Heywood, Chester D., *Negro Combat Troops in the World War: The Story of the 371st Infantry* (Worcester, Mass.: Commonwealth Press, 1928).

Jones, Lester M., "The Editorial Policy of Negro Newspapers of 1917-1918 as Compared with That of 1941-1942," *Journal of Negro History*, XXIX (January 1944).

Kennedy, Louise V., *The Negro Peasant Turns Cityward: Effects of Recent Migrations to Northern Centers* (New York: AMS Press, 1930).

Kerlin, Robert T., *The Voice of the Negro, 1919* (New York: E. P. Dutton & Co., 1920).

Little, Arthur W., *From Harlem to the Rhine: The Story of New York's Colored Volunteers* (New York: Covici, Friede, 1936).

Mecklin, John M., *The Ku Klux Klan: A Study of the American Mind* (New York: Harcourt, Brace & Co., 1924).

Moton, Robert R., *Finding A Way Out, An Autobiography* (New York: Doubleday & Co., 1920).

Scott, Emmett J., *The American Negro in the World War* (Chicago: Homewood Press, 1919).

_____, *Negro Migration During the War* (New York: Oxford University Press, 1920).

Smith, Lynn T., "The Redistribution of Negro Populations of the United States, 1910-1960," *Journal of Negro History*, LI (July 1966).

Williams, Charles H., *Sidelights on Negro Soldiers* (Boston: B. J. Brimmer Co., 1923).

25
Garveyism, Communism, and the "New Negro"

Bishop Henry McNeal Turner was the most outspoken black American advocate of black emigration between the Civil War and World War I. Edward Blyden, Martin R. Delaney, and Henry Highland Garnet were black emigrationists of some importance in the pre–Civil War era, the latter two having founded in 1854 the African Civilization Society which lasted until the Civil War. In 1901, Bishop Turner, pointing to the undoing of the Reconstruction as evidence that American blacks had no place in the United States, founded the Colored Emigration and Commercial Association "to purchase a . . . steamship for emigration and commercial purposes." Turner's intent was to consolidate the many small and relatively ineffective black emigration societies that had sprung up during the 1880s and 1890s into one effective association. However, because of strong black anti-emigration sentiment, the death of Bishop Turner in 1915, and World War I, the "all-consuming nationalism which demanded emigration to Africa" that was espoused by Turner was almost totally unsuccessful. It was Marcus Garvey who rekindled the black Americans' interest in going back to Africa.

THE GARVEY MOVEMENT

The Universal Negro Improvement Association (UNIA) was organized in

Jamaica by Marcus Moses Garvey in 1914 and had little success prior to Garvey's arrival in the United States in 1916. After his arrival, however, the UNIA took root and flourished. By 1919 the organization had 30 branches, 418 chartered divisions, and 422 divisions in the process of formation—an estimated membership of two million in the United States.

The basis for the tremendous growth in the United States was the severe conditions of exploitation and oppression under which the Afro-American masses suffered. Also, this was a time of hard economic conditions, of brutal lynchings and race riots. The UNIA offered a more obvious ray of hope than the NAACP and the Urban League.

The program of the UNIA was both national and international in character. The Preamble (1) condemned European nations for parceling up Africa and exploiting its people, (2) protested against the barbarous conditions of life of Afro-Americans in the West Indies and other colonial areas of the Western Hemisphere, and (3) denounced lynching, Jim Crow, race riots, discrimination in jobs and wage rates, inadequate education, denial of the right to vote, lack of justice in the courts, and the general state of terrorism under which Afro-Americans were compelled to live. Its Declaration of Rights demanded redress of the grievances of black people in various parts of the world and called upon them to (1) disregard all discriminatory laws, (2) use every available means to defend themselves from oppression, and (3) stop paying taxes to governments in which they were not represented.

One main theme of the Garvey Movement was "back to Africa." Garvey's position was actually rather ambiguous. He believed that black people should go to Africa. At the same time, he believed that black people should work to establish a strong African state that would serve as a protector for black people throughout the world. This suggests that he did not expect all black people to return to Africa. "To fight for African redemption," Garvey said, "does not mean that we must give up our domestic fights for political justice and industrial rights. It does not mean that we must become disloyal to any government or to any country wherein we were born . . . . We can be as loyal American citizens or British subjects as the Irishmen or the Jews, and yet fight for the redemption of Africa, a complete emancipation of the race. Fighting for the establishment of Palestine does not make the American Jew disloyal; fighting for the independence of Ireland does not make the Irish-American a bad citizen. Why should fighting for the freedom of Africa make the Afro-American disloyal or a bad citizen?"*

*Amy Jacques-Garvey, ed., *Philosophy and Opinions of Marcus Garvey* (New York: Universal Publishing House, 1923).

But Garvey did skillfully proceed to prepare for the actual transportation of Afro-Americans to Africa. With money solicited from blacks, he organized a steamship line, purchased two ships, and contracted for three others. A few voyages were made to Europe and Africa but with catastrophic financial losses. Eventually the enterprise collapsed.

While the financial debacle of the business enterprises of UNIA was taking place, the UNIA itself was going through a process of political decay. Garvey was shedding his radicalism and self-help philosophy and taking on a conservative point of view. This collided with the interests of many Afro-Americans. Garvey dropped his demands for Afro-American rights and concentrated everything upon his plan for a return to Africa. In doing so he appealed to white supremacist leaders for cooperation. The federal government, which conveniently ignored Afro-American lynchers and exploiters, indicted him for fraudulent use of the United States mails. In 1925 Garvey was found guilty and sentenced to five years in prison. He served two years after which he was pardoned and deported. (If nothing else, it should be recognized that Garvey was an outspoken black nationalist, and that the UNIA, before its change in political ideology, was the first militant black nationalist movement in the United States.)

The UNIA constituted a threat to the established Afro-American leadership, which denounced the organization as being the black counterpart of the American Colonization Society, demanded that Garvey be deported, and demanded the extirpation of the movement. Garvey was also attacked by his fellow West Indians.

After the disastrous business ventures and the change in political philosophy, the UNIA lost popular support, and by the early 1940s it had passed from the scene. But the movement did help give birth to a series of small groups such as the Forty-ninth State Movement, the Peace Movement for Ethiopia, the Black Muslims, and others.

THE COMMUNIST PARTY

As we have seen, the Socialist Party held to the theory that there was nothing special about the Afro-American question, that it was simply a part of the general problem of the working class. When the Communist Party came into being in the United States its program continued on this traditional line. It was not until 1921 that American Communists began to formulate a program concerning the Afro-American question as a specific one within the framework of Communist Party policy. The Party adopted a resolution stating that it would help blacks in their struggle for economic, political, and social equality and that it would seek to end the policy of discrimination followed by organized labor. Succeeding conventions expanded its program of specific Afro-American demands.

In 1928, the Communist Party adopted a resolution that characterized Afro-Americans in the Black Belt as an oppressed nation entitled to the right of self-determination. This change of policy came at a very difficult period for black Americans. There were race riots, widespread discrimination, lynching, and union ostracism. The Socialist Party ignored the Afro-American question, and the conservatively led NAACP and Urban League were not totally responsive to the struggles of the mass of Afro-Americans. As a consequence, Afro-Americans for the first time in their history began to join a Marxist organization—the Communist Party—for the Party was openly and vigorously advocating the right to work, the abolition of Jim Crowism, and full social equality.

The Communist Party carried on much of its Afro-American work directly through its own Party apparatus. During the national elections of 1932, 1936, and 1940, the Party's vice-presidential candidate was an Afro-American. Communists also raised the Afro-American question in the organizations in which they played a part. The Trade Union Educational League, the American Negro Labor Congress and the International Labor Defense, the League of Struggle for Negro Rights, the National Congress, and the Sharecroppers Union are only a few of the organizations that either were founded by the Communist Party or over which the Party had influence.

Despite these all-out efforts, the Communist Party made few Afro-American converts. In 1928 there were less than 200; in 1930 there were no more than 1500 members; and in 1932, out of 3973 Afro-Americans polled, only 51 planned to support the Communist nominees for national office. The majority of Afro-Americans were opposed to Communist concepts. Afro-Americans were not class conscious, they were radicals only on the race question, and they were somewhat suspicious of Communist Party leaders. Furthermore, the UNIA attracted some of the support that might otherwise have gone to the Communist Party.

THE "NEW NEGRO"

One of the important developments that took place in the Afro-American community was the acute awakening of a vast number of blacks to the tremendous discrepancies between the democratic rights and liberties as set forth in the Constitution and the enjoyment of these rights and liberties by the black community. Afro-Americans, especially during the post–World War I period, when thousands were being lynched, exploited, and otherwise oppressed, became extremely bitter and began to express their resentment in a variety of ways. This period in Afro-American history is known as the Harlem Renaissance, the Black Renaissance, or the New Negro Movement.

For the most part, the literature of the Black Renaissance protested segregation, discrimination, and terrorism, and demanded first-class citizenship. New York, long the center of Afro-American intellectual and cultural life in America, was teeming with authors, playwrights, painters, sculptors, singers, actors, and musicians. While New York was the incubator of the movement, it could not claim a monopoly on Afro-American protest during these times. Gradually the scope of the movement came to include the whole of the United States. Poetry circles, little theaters, and so forth could be found in every sizable city in the United States.

Before the movement Afro-American writers and actors had to confine their words and actions to expressions that were allegedly "black," e.g., foot shuffling, *da*'s and *dis*'s. But with the advent of the "New Negro," it was no longer necessary for Afro-American actors and singers to assume only those roles that were acceptable to white audiences. Afro-American artists began to receive worldwide recognition, and white painters began to give serious attention to Afro-American subjects. In other areas (movies, concert stage, sports, and science) Afro-Americans demonstrated both their talent and their determination not to accept the color line. They demanded to be seen and heard and recognized as human beings by white Americans.

The "New Negro" who came into focus after the close of World War I did not disappear. The great economic depression and World War II did not interrupt the movement but actually stimulated the Afro-American, for with greater educational opportunities and more economic security blacks had less fear of self-expression and self-revelation.

REFERENCES

Bontemps, Arna, ed., *The Harlem Renaissance Remembered* (New York: Dodd, Mead and Co., 1972).

Clarke, John Henrik, *Harlem, A Community in Transition* (New York: Citadel Press, 1964).

Cronon, David E., *Black Moses: The Story of Marcus Garvey and the Universal Negro Improvement Association* (Madison, Wisc.: University of Wisconsin Press, 1955).

Garvey, Amy J., *Philosophy and Opinions of Marcus Garvey* (New York: Universal Publishing House, 1923).

Gloster, H. M., *Negro Voices in American Fiction* (Chapel Hill, N.C.: University of North Carolina Press, 1948).

Holden, Edith, *Blyden of Liberia: An Account of the Life and Labor of Edward Wilmot Blyden L.L.D.* (New York: Oxford University Press, 1966).

*Hughes, Langston, *The Big Sea* (New York: Alfred A. Knopf, 1940 [Hill & Wang]).

Locke, Alain, *The Negro in Art* (Washington, D.C.: Associates in Negro Folk Education, 1940).

*_____, ed., *The New Negro: An Interpretation* (New York: A. & C. Boni, 1925 [Atheneum]).

Lynch, Hollis R., *Edward Wilmot Blyden, Pan-Negro Patriot 1832-1912* (London: Oxford University Press, 1967).

Meier, August, *Negro Thought in America, 1880-1915* (Ann Arbor: University of Michigan Press, 1963).

Noble, Peter, *The Negro in Films* (London: S. Robinson, 1948).

*Osofsky, Gilbert, *Harlem: The Making of a Ghetto* (New York: Harper & Row, 1966 [Torchbook, Harper & Row]).

Ponton, Mungo M., *The Life and Times of Bishop Henry M. Turner* (Atlanta: Negro University, 1971).

Record, Wilson, *The Negro and the Communist Party* (Chapel Hill, N.C.: University of North Carolina Press, 1951).

*_____, *Race and Radicalism: The NAACP and the Communist Party in Conflict* (Ithaca, N.Y.: Cornell University Press, 1964 [Cornell University Press]).

Redkey, Edwin S., *Black Exodus* (New Haven: Yale University Press, 1969).

Scheiner, Seth M., *Negro Mecca: A History of the Negro in New York City, 1865-1920* (New York: New York University Press, 1965).

Staudenraus, Philip J., *The African Colonization Movement, 1816-1865* (New York: Columbia University, 1961).

Thorpe, Earl E., *The Mind of the Negro: An Intellectual History of Afro-Americans* (Baton Rouge, La.: Ortlieb Press, 1961).

Vincent, Theodore G., *Black Power and the Garvey Movement* (Berkeley: Ramparts Press, 1971).

Young, James O., *Black Writers of the Thirties* (Baton Rouge: Louisiana State University Press, 1973).

26
The Economic Crisis and the New Deal

THE ECONOMIC CRISIS

The economic crisis of 1929 through 1933 wrecked the economy of the United States. Over $160 billion in stocks were wiped out, industrial production fell by 50 percent, 5761 banks closed. The value of farm products dropped from $8.5 billion to $4 billion, wages were cut by at least 45 percent, and the total number of unemployed reached seventeen million by March 1933.

Afro-Americans suffered most during the crisis. In the industrial centers unemployment among blacks ran twice as high as whites: Afro-Americans were laid off and whites given their jobs. Wages for Afro-Americans averaged 30 percent less than those for whites. Discrimination in relief distribution was endemic. Stipends for Afro-Americans were generally lower, and many were denied assistance altogether. Always the poorest paid, blacks had little or no reserves with which to meet the crisis. Living conditions were beyond description. This desperate situation gave rise to hunger marches and demonstrations all over the United States. There were several large national marches. Black Americans also organized cooperatives, "Jobs-For-Negro" boycotts, and rent strikes.

Disgusted with Hoover's policies, the electorate swept Franklin D. Roosevelt into the Presidency in 1932. Strong Afro-American support for the Roosevelt Democracy represented a decisive shift away from the Republican Party, which Afro-Americans had supported faithfully since the Reconstruction Era. The promise of the New Deal and Roosevelt's personal interest kept the black voters solidly within the Democratic Party in succeeding elections.

AFRO-AMERICAN ORGANIZATIONS

Organized and militant movements were in part produced by some of the same social conditions that had made for political change. One was the Southern Negro Youth Congress, organized in February 1937. For over a decade, 1937–1948, there were few battles of the southern blacks in which this organization did not play a role. In addition, the Southern Conference for Human Welfare, founded in November 1938, brought together southern white liberals and Afro-Americans for the first time since the days of Populism in the 1890s.

The National Negro Congress, founded in February 1936, was a federation of organizations representing black Republicans and Democrats, Socialists and Communists, professionals and laborers, and church and civic groups. The Congress operated in the tradition of the historic Afro-American convention movement of antebellum times. By and large, all of these organizations condemned Jim Crow, lynching, and the poll tax. They advocated trade union unity, adequate relief for unemployed blacks, abolition of sharecropping, and the establishment of cooperatives.

Most of these groups faded away during the 1940s. Some of their demands had been incorporated into the platforms of national political parties. Attention shifted toward international issues. And most significant, the expanding army and war economy alleviated much of the black people's immediate economic misery.

THE NEW DEAL

The New Deal was an attempt to repair the existing economic system of the United States. The New Deal proposed to (a) reconstruct the banking system, (b) rescue business with loans and subsidies, (c) stimulate private investment, (d) raise prices by setting inflationary tendencies into operation, (e) overcome agricultural overproduction by acreage reduction and crop destruction, (f) protect against mortgage foreclosure, (g) create employment and stimulate purchasing power through public works programs, and (h) provide relief for the unemployed and the unemployable. The New Deal program did not prevent the continuation of Jim Crow policies by local administrations, but Afro-Americans generally benefited. Although frequently cheated in the allotment of cash benefits under the Agricultural Adjustment Administration for plowing crops under, a few black farmers did receive some cash benefits. The Tennessee Valley Authority and the Rural Electrification Administration brought electricity to some rural Afro-American homes for the first time. Loans from the Farm Security Administration and the Home Owners Loan Corporation enabled blacks to purchase farms and homes. The housing authorities built low-cost projects and thereby, for the first time in United States history, provided decent homes for black Americans on an extensive basis. Some blacks learned trades and others continued their education under the National Youth Administration. Others learned to read while in the Civilian Conservation Corps. Unemployed actors, artists, and writers found relief through the Work Projects Administration.

Unfortunately blacks were largely left out of the social welfare program. The Social Security Act of 1935 exempted agricultural and domestic labor. Unemployment compensation was administered by the states. Blacks, especially in the South, failed to benefit.

ROOSEVELT'S BLACK CABINET

One of the most important developments of the New Deal era was the establishment of the "Black Cabinet." Previous Presidents had occasionally listened to the advice of an Afro-American leader, but Roosevelt, to the outrage of the southern wing of the Democratic Party, gathered around him many prominent Afro-Americans, including Robert L. Vann, William H. Hastie, Robert C. Weaver, Eugene Kinckle Jones, L. A. Oxley, Mary McLeod Bethune, and others. Although none was entrusted with major executive positions, such Afro-Americans were prominent in the New Deal administration and advised Roosevelt on ways of seeking economic, political, and civil equality for Afro-Americans.

Even though there was a significant increase in the number of Afro-Americans employed by the federal government, the New Deal administration, with its Black Cabinet, did very little to eradicate the burning grievances of the black masses: Nothing was done by the administration to pass federal anti-lynching legislation or to abolish the poll tax, to end discrimination in the armed services, or to prevent the gross inequality in the education of blacks and whites. The Afro-American community, despite the reforms and the expenditure of some $40 million, suffered from mass unemployment, police brutality, job and relief discrimination, wretched housing, and bad medical and educational facilities. It was only with the outbreak of World War II, when the economy of the United States went back into full operation, that the Afro-American community received some relief.

REFERENCES

Goshell, Harold F., *Negro Politicians: The Rise of Negro Politics in Chicago* (Chicago: University of Chicago Press, 1935).

Hayes, Laurence J. W., *The Negro Federal Government Worker: A Study of His Classification Status in the District of Columbia, 1883-1938* (Washington, D.C.: Howard University Studies in Social Sciences, 1941).

Ottley, Roi, *"New World A-Coming," Inside Black America* (New York: World Publishing Co., 1943).

*Powdermaker, Hortense, *After Freedom: A Cultural Study in the Deep South* (New York: Atheneum, 1968 [Atheneum]).

Sterner, Richard, et al., *The Negro's Share: A Study of Income, Consumption, Housing, and Public Assistance* (New York: Harper & Bros., 1943).

Van Deusen, John G., *The Black Man in White America* (Washington, D.C.: Associated Publishers, Inc., 1944).

Walters, Raymond, *Negroes and the Great Depression* (Westport, Conn.: Greenwood Publishing Corp., 1970).

Wright, Marian T., "Negro Youth and the Federal Emergency Programs: CCC and NYA," *Journal of Negro Education*, IX (July 1940).

27
New Trade Unionism

At the beginning of the New Deal, most AF of L and unaffiliated unions still excluded Afro-Americans from membership, either in their constitutions or by local practice. Some unions reserved an auxiliary status for Afro-Americans virtually tantamount to exclusion. Labor officials not only kept Afro-Americans from becoming union members but also often kept the few who did become members from getting jobs in industry. As late as 1941 the AF of L justified its Jim Crow policies by arguing that discrimination existed before the AF of L was born and human nature could not be altered.

The policies of the Railroad Brotherhoods—engineers, firemen, conductors, trainmen, and switchmen—were especially anti-black. They succeeded in keeping Afro-Americans out of the operating and mechanical trades in the North, restricting them almost exclusively to the occupations of porters, waiters, and common laborers. In the South, where Afro-Americans were employed in all of the railroad trades, the growing Brotherhoods started a vigorous campaign to make the southern railroads as lily-white as those in the North. By 1933 southern Afro-Americans had been eliminated from all operating and mechanical jobs.

In retaliation, black railroad workers attempted to form separate unions, but with the exception of the Pullman Porters, which was organized in 1925, they never succeeded. Black leaders differed on the trade union question. While some agitated for the unionization of black workers, many others were quite cold on the matter.

Strong pressures were being generated for broader organization. After a resolution proposing industrial unionization failed to pass the AF of L Convention of 1935, eight unions left to form the Committee for Industrial Organization, with a program for unionizing the basic industries. Despite efforts by the AF of L to defeat it, the organizing campaign of the CIO was a success from the start. Workers poured into the new industrial unions. The CIO's growth even forced the AF of L to organize more intensively: Some of its constituent unions opened their ranks to those outside narrow craft lines, and a few even became virtual industrial unions along the pattern established by the CIO.

Afro-Americans readily entered the unions despite the outrageous way they had been "Jim Crow'd" by the AF of L and notwithstanding the opposition of many black leaders. It is estimated that in 1930 there were 110,000 black union members; 180,000 in 1935; and 1,150,000 in 1948 (650,000 in the AF of L and 500,000 in the CIO).

From the outset, the CIO took a positive attitude toward the organization of Afro-Americans. Its national constitution called for the effective organization of workingmen, regardless of race, creed, color, or nationality, and all the affiliated unions were supposed to follow this general policy. Nevertheless, discrimination against black members existed in the CIO and its affiliates. Although black workers accumulated seniority rights, they were still the last to be hired and the first to be fired. Afro-Americans in industries organized by these CIO unions filled a disproportionate percentage of the lower paid, unskilled jobs. Efforts to upgrade and promote them to better jobs were totally inadequate. Afro-Americans did not hold high official union posts. To be sure, the CIO unions had official anti-discrimination committees and sometimes wrote anti-discrimination clauses into union contracts, but usually only lip service was paid to the application of either.

The AF of L lagged considerably behind even the modest gains established in the CIO. Many craft unions maintained their exclusionary policies intact.

The Roosevelt Administration passed several important labor laws that eventually benefited Afro-American workers. One was the National Labor Relations Act of 1935, which conceded to workers the right to organize, to bargain collectively, and to elect union representatives of their own choosing. Another was the Fair Labor Standards Act of 1938, which established the forty-hour week and a minimum national wage. This law established minimum wages for about a million Afro-American workers in industry, but it excluded the majority of Afro-Americans who were engaged in agriculture and domestic service. Another measure affecting Afro-Americans more than any other was the law that established the Fair Employment Practices Committee, set up to implement Roosevelt's Executive Order No. 8802 of June 1941. The order stated that there shall be no discrimination in the employment of workers in defense industries or Government because of race, creed, color, or national origin.

The FEPC horrified white southerners. The CIO openly endorsed the measure, while the AF of L and Railroad Brotherhoods eyed it suspiciously. Even though the national conventions of all these unions endorsed the order, they refused to discipline their affiliated unions, which continued to discriminate against Afro-American workers. At the outset of World War II, racial bias in industry was almost universal.

REFERENCES

Brazeal, Brailsford R., *The Brotherhood of Sleeping Car Porters; Its Origin and Development* (New York: Harper & Bros., 1946).

Cayton, Horace, and George S. Mitchell, *Black Workers and the New Unions* (Chapel Hill, N.C.: University of North Carolina Press, 1939).

Greene, Lorenzo, and Carter G. Woodson, *The Negro Wage Earner* (Washington, D.C.: Association for the Study of Negro Life & History, 1930).

*Jacobsen, Julius, *The Negro and the American Labor Movement* (New York: Doubleday & Co., 1968 [Anchor]).

Johnson, Charles S., *The Economic Status of Negroes* (Nashville, Tenn.: Fisk Union Press, 1933).

Marshall, Ray, *The Negro and Apprenticeship* (Baltimore, Md.: Johns Hopkins University Press, 1967).

————, *The Negro and Organized Labor* (New York: Wiley, 1965).

*————, *The Negro Worker* (New York: Random House, 1967 [Random House]).

Northrup, Herbert R., *Organized Labor and the Negro* (New York: Harper & Bros., 1944).

Rosengarten, Theodore, *All God's Dangers: The Life of Nate Shaw* (New York: Alfred A. Knopf, 1974).

Ross, Arthur M., and Herbert Hill, eds., *Employment, Race, and Poverty* (New York: Harcourt, Brace & World, 1967).

*Spero, Sterling D., and Abram L. Harris, *The Black Worker: The Negro and the Labor Movement* (Port Washington, N.Y.: Kennikat Press, 1966 [Atheneum]).

Sterner, Richard, *et al.*, *The Negro's Share: A Study of Income, Consumption, Housing and Public Assistance* (New York: Harper & Bros., 1943).

Weaver, Robert C., *Negro Labor, A National Problem* (New York: Harcourt, Brace & Co., 1946).

28
Supreme Court Decisions

From colonial times through the first half of the twentieth century, the attitude of the United States Supreme Court seems to have been that of a large segment of the American body politic who supported or condoned the institution of slavery, who believed in the inherent inferiority of Afro-Americans, and who believed that whites and blacks could never live peaceably together in the United States. It was a small minority, the abolitionists and radical Republicans, who advocated equal political, civil, economic, and social rights for Afro-Americans. Public sentiment certainly influenced the Court's decisions concerning the rights of blacks and their status in American life.

Soon after the first blacks arrived in North America to perform servile labor, colonial courts, and later state and federal courts, dealt with cases concerning their rights, duties, and status. Generally, the courts held that slaves had no rights, that they were chattel property subject to the complete domination of their masters. The courts upheld the laws that governed the conduct of the slaves and the so-called free blacks.

The first Supreme Court case that had nationwide repercussions was the Dred Scott decision of 1857. Handed down during the critical years prior to the Civil War, the decision legally opened all American territories to slavery. It also held that blacks were inferior to whites and "could be justly and lawfully reduced to slavery for his benefit." "He had no rights which the white man was bound to respect." Even if franchised, blacks could not become citizens.

Not until after the Civil War did the Supreme Court begin to deal systematically with the problems of black people. During the 1870s and 1880s the Court steadily whittled away at the civil rights secured from the radical Congress and reconstructed state governments.

1. Slaughter House Cases (1873)—The Court ruled that most privileges and immunities inhered in state citizenship and thus were not protected by the Fourteenth Amendment.
2. *U.S.* vs. *Cruikshank* and *U.S.* vs. *Reese* (1876)—Ruled unconstitutional the critical sections of the Enforcement Act of 1870, which protected the civil rights of citizens as guaranteed by the U.S. Constitution, especially the Thirteenth, Fourteenth, and Fifteenth Amendments.
3. *Hall* vs. *DeCuir* (1878)—Invalidated a Louisiana statute prohibiting segregation in interstate commerce as an undue burden on such trade.
4. *U.S.* vs. *Harris* (1883)—Struck down sections of the Ku Klux Klan Act of 1871, which penalized persons conspiring to impede the Fourteenth and Fifteenth Amendments.
5. Civil Rights Cases (1883)—Voided the Civil Rights Act of 1875, the last serious attempt to provide equality for blacks.
6. *Plessy* vs. *Ferguson* (1896)—Held that separate-but-equal facilities did not violate the Thirteenth and Fourteenth Amendments.

It was only after 1910 that the Supreme Court began to make good on some of the promises of the Civil War amendments to the Constitution.

1. *Bailey* vs. *Alabama* (1911)—Declared that peonage violated the Thirteenth Amendment.
2. *Guinn* vs. *U.S.* (1915)—Invalidated the Oklahoma "Grandfather Clause."
3. *Buchanan* vs. *Warley* (1917)—Held that a Louisville, Kentucky, ordinance providing for residential segregation violated the Fourteenth Amendment.
4. *Corrigan* vs. *Buckley* (1926)—Represented the primacy of property rights over civil rights. The Court held that restrictive covenants in property transactions were not subject to litigation.
5. *Nixon* vs. *Herndon* (1927) and *Nixon* vs. *Condon* (1932)—En-

joined the state of Texas from providing for a white primary election through statute.

6. *Powell* vs. *Alabama* (1932)—Established that the necessity of counsel was so vital and imperative that the failure of the trial court to make an effective appointment of counsel was a denial of due process of law within the meaning of the Fourteenth Amendment. This decision eventually led to the freeing of nine Scottsboro boys accused of raping two white girls.

7. *Grovey* vs. *Townsend* (1935)—Sustained the exclusion of blacks from the Texas primary on grounds that the state Democratic Convention was not an arm of the state.

8. *Norris* vs. *Alabama* (1935)—Indicated that the exclusion of Afro-Americans and other minorities from juries was prima facie evidence of discrimination.

9. *New Negro Alliance* vs. *Sanitary Grocery Company* (1938)— Held that a picket line of black people was a labor dispute within the meaning of the Norris-LaGuardia Act of 1932.

10. *Missouri ex rel Gaines* vs. *Canada* (1938)—Required states with separate school systems to provide substantially equal facilities for blacks.

11. *Mitchell* vs. *United States* (1941)—Was the first of a series of decisions in which the Court struck down segregation in interstate commerce.

12. *Smith* vs. *Allwright* (1944)—Reversed the Court's position by declaring the white primary unconstitutional.

Constitutional developments through the end of World War II represented something of a start for Afro-Americans on the road to full legal citizenship. In 1941 the Justice Department established a division to investigate and prosecute civil rights violations. Yet the pace of change, and the continued resistance, indicated that the struggle would be long and difficult.

REFERENCES

Greenberg, Jack, *Race Relations and American Law* (New York: Columbia University Press, 1959).
Harris, Robert J., *The Quest for Equality* (Baton Rouge, La.: Louisiana State University Press, 1960).

*Hopkins, Vincent, *Dred Scott's Case* (New York: Russell & Russell, 1951 [Atheneum, 1967]).

Kelly, Alfred, "The Congressional Controversy Over School Segregation, 1867-1875," *American Historical Review*, LXIV (April 1959).

*Konvitz, Milton, and Theodore Leskes, *A Century of Civil Rights* (New York: Columbia University Press, 1961 [Columbia University Press]).

Levy, Leonard, and Harlan Phillips, "The Roberts Case: Source of the Separate but Equal Doctrine," *American Historical Review*, LVI (April 1951).

*Nichols, Roy, *The Disruption of American Democracy* (New York: The Macmillan Co., 1948 [Free Press]).

Swinney, Everett, "Enforcing the Fifteenth Amendment, 1870-1877," *Journal of Southern History*, XXVIII (May 1962).

*Woodward, C. Vann, *Reunion and Reaction* (Boston: Little, Brown and Co., 1951 [Little]).

————, "The South and the Law of the Land: The Present Resistance and Its Prospects," *Commentary*, XXVI (November 1958).

*————, *The Strange Career of Jim Crow* (New York: Oxford University Press, 1955 [Oxford University Press]).

29
The Afro-American and World War II

PRE-WAR YEARS

In the pre-war struggle against fascism, Afro-Americans played a very active part. Long familiar with racist slander, they were openly maligned by Nazi propagandists as subhumans. They understood the dangers of fascism in an intimate way. Black Americans resented Hitler's insulting the black members of the American Olympic team in Berlin in 1936, while they cheered Joe Louis' knockout of the Nazi heavyweight Max Schmeling two years later.

Many Afro-Americans took an active part in the anti-war demonstrations. Others supported the Republican cause in Spain. A Negro People's Committee to Aid Spanish Democracy was formed. Some joined the International Brigades. Afro-Americans were particularly angered by Mussolini's attack and conquest of Ethiopia in 1935. Protest meetings and demonstrations were held; committees were formed, which collected money and other aid for the beleaguered Ethiopians. These Afro-Americans also lodged a protest with the League of Nations, but to no avail.

AFRO-AMERICANS IN THE WAR

In 1940 less than 10,000 Afro-Americans were in the armed forces. The

Army had less than 5000, while the Navy had some 4000. Only four black units in the Regular Army were up to full strength, and these were staffed by less than a dozen black officers. Both the Air Corps and the Marines were lily-white.

In October 1940 the War Department announced that blacks would be drafted into the Army in proportion to population. White and black soldiers, however, were to be segregated. Despite segregation, most Afro-Americans were pleased with nondiscriminatory draft procedures. More than 3,000,000 Afro-Americans registered when the Selective Service System was established in 1940. Only 2,069 blacks were drafted in the remaining months of 1940. In the following year, 100,000 entered the military, and the figure swelled to 370,000 in 1942. By the end of the war, when the armed forces were at their peak, nearly a million blacks were in the service. There were 701,678 in the Army, 165,000 in the Navy, 17,000 in the Marines, and 900 in the Coast Guard. In addition, approximately 24,000 were in the Merchant Marine.

The deployment of black troops overseas constituted a major problem for the War Department. Most foreign countries did not want black troops for reasons ranging from miscegenation to economics. Australia and Panama, for example, had "white only" immigration policies. Britain and France feared that the presence of black American troops would disrupt their control over blacks in their African and West Indian colonies. Many white American officers were also opposed to the use of black soldiers in their commands. As demands for the withdrawal of black troops mounted and requests that no black troops be sent flowed in, a definite policy had to be worked out. After refusing to withdraw black troops except in cases of extreme necessity, it was decided that black troops who performed service-type duties would be acceptable. Ultimately, military considerations and very serious problems of morale and race relations in military camps in the United States forced the War Department to send considerable numbers of black service and combat troops abroad. The pressure of Afro-American opinion and the large numbers of fresh draftees were also major factors in determining the use of black soldiers in the various overseas theaters of operations.

Afro-American Officers
The question of Afro-American officers had always plagued the government. As war became imminent, Afro-Americans were determined to secure equal and integrated officer training. In 1940 the War Department had planned to admit both white and black officer candidates to the same schools, but the

reluctance of commanders to recommend blacks for training forced Washington to issue a special order that all selections be made without discrimination. By the middle of 1942 some two hundred blacks were being commissioned each month. Nevertheless, problems remained in the assignment of these junior officers. Since they were limited to service in black units, many regiments became overstocked with officers. Both white and black women also trained together in the Women's Auxiliary Army Corps, and few problems seemed to have developed with the integration of its training facilities.

The Navy had no Afro-American officers until 1944. By the end of the war about fifty blacks, men and women, served as ensigns and lieutenants in several support capacities. Only a handful of blacks were commissioned in the Marines and the Coast Guard.

The success of mixed officer-candidate schools had no influence on pilot training. A separate aviation school for Afro-American cadets was set up at Tuskegee Institute, and approximately six hundred Afro-American pilots had received their wings by the end of the war.

In the Army
Although black troops were segregated, they had a greater opportunity to serve their country than in any previous war. But as usual they were still heavily concentrated in the support branches. In 1942 nearly one-half of the black soldiers were in service units. The proportion rose to three-fourths by mid-1945.

Afro-American troops were sent to all theaters of the war. From Iceland to Kenya, Trinidad to China, India to Alaska, black soldiers built highways, bridges, and airports, unloaded ships, drove supply trucks to the front lines, rebuilt cities, and performed other invaluable support services. Their level of performance—often under the hostile glare of the white army—approached the heroic. Many handled weapons with skill and courage when called upon. The Battle of the Bulge was the most notable example. The combat record reveals some of the problems of morale that were created by segregation. But considering racism, poor training, and bad leadership, the performance of black troops was excellent, according to the Chief of the Army's Historical Office in 1946.

In the eastward offensive into Germany the need for infantry replacements became so acute that an order was issued to re-train service troops and assign them to combat units regardless of race. A subsequent directive forestalled complete integration, but black platoons were placed on the line in white units, where they fought with conspicuous valor.

In the Navy

When the war commenced, most Afro-Americans in the Navy were mess men. Two months before Pearl Harbor the Navy announced that this policy would be maintained for new recruits. Pressure from blacks and liberal whites, however, forced the Navy to alter its Jim Crow policy. By the Spring of 1942 the Navy acceded to demands that black enlistees be used for general duties, but it steadfastly refused to assign Afro-American sailors to combat vessels. They would be utilized on shore installations and harbor craft and trained and placed in separate units. Afro-Americans were enraged and protests increased. The black press, civilian leaders, clergymen, and servicemen held demonstrations, hunger strikes, and refused to obey orders.

The protests finally forced concessions. In February 1944 the Navy announced that two ships would be manned by Afro-American crews with white officers. Two months later twenty-two blacks were commissioned as officers. By August, Afro-Americans were being assigned to auxiliary ships in several service capacities. Subsequently, black sailors were assigned to all fleet auxiliaries. At the same time training camps and technical schools were integrated, but not until after the war were all racial restrictions on assignments finally lifted.

The Coast Guard began accepting Afro-Americans for various service jobs in May 1942. Its history of abolishing Jim Crow policies followed that of the Navy.

The Marine Corps accepted Afro-Americans for the first time in its 167-year history in June 1942. While they were accepted in all capacities, their combat duties were limited to guarding secured areas.

Although the WAVES and SPARS, the women's contingents of the Navy and Coast Guard, were organized in 1942, black women were excluded until late in 1944. Pressure from black public opinion and especially from Afro-American women's organizations was instrumental in breaking down the barrier. The Marine Corps never accepted Afro-American women.

In the Merchant Marine

The Merchant Marine was integrated from the start of hostilities, with Afro-Americans serving in all job categories. Four Liberty ships were commanded by black captains, and eighteen ships were named after outstanding Afro-Americans and black seamen who died in active service. This non-Jim Crow policy derived directly from the civilian character of the Merchant Marine and from its tradition of employing blacks as well as whites.

ON THE HOME FRONT

When the national defense program commenced in 1940, most defense contractors employed no blacks except in the most menial and unskilled jobs. A national advisory commission was appointed to study the matter. After much investigation it recommended that such contractors adopt nondiscriminatory employment practices. These recommendations were ignored despite severe labor shortages in many areas. White workers were being imported into industrial centers where qualified Afro-Americans were seeking jobs. Only 4500 out of 175,000 persons training under the National Defense Training Act were black, even though discrimination was forbidden by statute.

Afro-Americans and liberal whites vigorously protested this blatant racism in the war industries. Unable to get results through negotiations, a national protest march on Washington by 100,000 people was planned for July 1941. A. Philip Randolph, head of the Brotherhood of Sleeping Car Porters, resisted the advice of white liberals to back down, declaring that the march would take place if no action was forthcoming. Under the threat of the march, Roosevelt issued an executive order in June that (1) affirmed the government's policy of equal job opportunity, (2) directed that the vocational training program be conducted without bias, (3) stipulated that all government contracts include a clause prohibiting discrimination, and (4) established a Committee on Fair Employment to investigate violations of the order.

Results came quickly. Rather than face public investigations, defense contractors began to hire Afro-Americans. By October 1944 some 325,000 blacks had received some type of vocational training. By 1944 one million more Afro-Americans held civilian jobs than in 1940. The number of black federal employees soared from 60,000 to 300,000. In 1940 only 4.4 percent of male black workers were in skilled categories compared to 7.3 percent in 1944. During the same period the number of black semi-skilled workers nearly doubled. Economically, the war was a triumph for black labor. More jobs at better wages were available. Many trades and industries, previously restricted to whites, were opened.

The war also produced enormous demographic changes. The tempo of northward migration, which had been steadily increasing since Reconstruction, rapidly accelerated. Nearly 1,500,000 blacks left the South for the burgeoning war industries in the North and on the West Coast between 1940 and 1950. Migration to the West Coast occurred for the first time. Over 250,000 black people moved to California to work in the aviation and shipbuilding industries. The exodus from the South had become a major demographic trend by 1950, which was to continue regardless of economic conditions.

The bright outlook in employment was dimmed by racist patterns in social relations. Afro-Americans were particularly disturbed by the treatment of black troops in communities where their camps were located. These soldiers were subjected to white hostility and often to violence. Blacks were also concerned over the race problems that were developing in the urban centers, north and south. Rapidly increasing population and competition for jobs and housing engendered racial tensions. Fights and riots frequently resulted. These outbreaks led to the establishment of various human relations commissions. But more significantly, they showed that black Americans were still faced with hostility and discrimination.

REFERENCES

Anderson, Jervis, A. *Philip Randolph: A Biographical Portrait* (New York: Harcourt Brace Jovanovich, Inc. 1973).

Brown, Earl, "American Negroes and the War," *Harper's Magazine,* CLXXXIV (April 1942).

Clark, Kenneth B., "Morale of the Negro on the Home Front," *Journal of Negro Education,* XII (Summer 1943).

Dalfiume, Richard, "The Forgotten Years of the Negro Revolution," *Journal of American History,* LV (June 1968).

Francis, Charles E., *The Tuskegee Airmen: The Story of the Negro in the U.S. Air Force* (Boston: Bruce Humphries, 1955).

Jones, Lester M., "The Editorial Policy of Negro Newspapers of 1917-1918 as Compared with That of 1941-1942," *Journal of Negro History,* XXXIX (January 1944).

Lee, Ulysses, *United States Army in World War II: The Deployment of Negro Troops* (Washington, D.C.: Office of the Chief of Military History, U.S. Army, 1966).

Paszek, Lawrence J., "Negroes and the Air Force, 1939-1949," *Military Affairs* (Spring 1967).

Schoenfield, Seymour J., *The Negro in the Armed Forces* (Washington, D.C.: Associated Publishers, Inc., 1945).

Silvera, John D., *The Negro in World War II* (Baton Rouge, La.: Military Press, Inc., 1946).

White, Walter, *A Rising Wind* (Garden City, N.Y.: Doubleday, Doran & Co., 1945).

30
The Struggle for Civil Rights

Black Americans were quite fortunate to have Harry S Truman succeed Franklin D. Roosevelt as President. Based upon the findings and recommendations of his advisory Committee on Civil Rights early in 1948, Truman requested the enactment of the first comprehensive civil rights legislation in the twentieth century calling for anti-lynching, anti-poll tax, public accommodations, fair employment, voting and equal rights legislation. Congress, however, did not pass a civil rights bill until 1957; although it was a modest bill, it was the forerunner of the civil rights legislation of 1960, 1964, 1965, 1968, and 1972.

VOTING RIGHTS

The Civil Rights Act of 1957 attempted to guarantee blacks the right to vote by authorizing the Justice Department to initiate court proceedings to counter irregularities in federal elections. However, the United States Commission on Civil Rights, which was established in 1957 and only given authority to investigate allegations of voting irregularities, reported in 1959 that stronger measures of enforcement were necessary to guarantee voting rights. The Commission recommended the appointment of federal registrars to register voters in places where it was determined that state registrars had refused to register qualified voters because of race, religion, or national origin.

Although requested in 1948, it was not until 1960 that Congress finally approved the Twenty-fourth Amendment, banning the poll tax in federal elections. Ratified in 1964, the amendment only affected five states (Alabama, Arkansas, Mississippi, Texas, and Virginia); however, these states, by using the poll tax and other devices, had successfully prevented thousands of blacks from voting.

In addition, Congress included provisions in the Civil Rights Act of 1960 calling for court enforcement of voting rights where there were "patterns" of discrimination and requiring states to preserve all federal voting and registration records.

In spite of these laws, in 1963 the Commission on Civil Rights again reported that the Civil Rights Acts of 1957 and 1960 failed to provide effective measures to prevent the "widespread denials of the right to vote." The result was the enactment of the most comprehensive piece of civil rights legislation in the nation's history, the Civil Rights Act of 1964. This Act, as it pertained to voting rights, prohibited different voting registration requirements for state and federal elections and made a sixth-grade education a rebuttable presumption of literacy.

Because of the tragic events surrounding the voter registration marches from Selma to Montgomery, Alabama, Congress was convinced that additional federal legislation was necessary to guarantee blacks the right to vote. Accordingly, Congress passed the Voting Rights Act of 1965 which (1) gave the U.S. Attorney General the power to appoint federal examiners to supervise voter registration in states or voting districts "where a literacy or other qualifying test was in use or where fewer than 50 percent of voting age residents were registered or had voted in 1964"; (2) established criminal penalties for interfering with persons exercising their right to vote; and (3) prohibited states from imposing new voter qualification laws unless such laws were approved by a federal court. Only eight states were affected by the Voting Rights Act of 1965 (Alabama, Alaska, Georgia, Louisiana, Mississippi, North Carolina, South Carolina, and Virginia), but it further guaranteed hundreds of thousands of blacks the right to exercise their franchise.

The Civil Rights Act of 1968 also strengthened this right by including provisions which protected from intimidation or injury persons who exercised their right to vote or who ran for political office.

Responding to the opportunity to register and vote, southern blacks have elected a number of federal, state, county, and local officials. From

1960 to the summer-fall of 1969, the number of black registered voters in the eleven ex-Confederate states increased the number of black registered voters from 1,463,333 to 3,248,000; Mississippi experienced the most spectacular increase in black voters, from 22,000 in 1960 to 281,000 in 1968. The high point of these efforts was the election of a black, Maynard Jackson, as mayor of Atlanta, Georgia, in 1973.

Taking notice of the political strength of southern blacks, southern white officeholders began adding blacks to their staffs and otherwise "courting" the black vote. In November 1973 Alabama Governor George C. Wallace, once the symbol of southern segregation, spoke at a southern black mayors' conference in Tuskegee. In April of the following year Tuskegee's black mayor, Johnny Ford, endorsed Wallace for reelection and predicted that Wallace would carry Macon County where blacks constituted 83 percent of the population.

During the civil rights years Washington, D.C., blacks, who comprise a majority of the District's population, and their black, federally appointed mayor, Walter Washington, intensified their efforts to achieve home-rule. Federal legislation before Congress in 1974 called for the "election" of a mayor and a thirteen-member council to govern the District.

Blacks in the North, East, and West also began to display political interest. While approximately 1,350,000 Afro-Americans had migrated to the urban centers outside the South during the 1950s, they, together with those who had migrated during World War II, had not exercised their right to vote. Spurred on by the massive voter registration drive, get-out-the-vote activity in the South, and a growing voter-awareness of the potential to control cities as a result of whites fleeing to the suburbs, blacks in the urban centers began to register and vote. The results have been as astonishing as they were in the South. As of April 1973 only six states—Hawaii, Idaho, Montana, North Dakota, South Dakota, and Utah—had fewer than five elected black officials. Undoubtedly the election which received the greatest national attention was the election in 1973 of Thomas Bradley, black son of a Texas sharecropper, as the mayor of Los Angeles, the third largest city in the United States.

EMPLOYMENT

With the cutback in war-related jobs after World War II, blacks lost their jobs more rapidly than whites. Fortunately there was a concurrent peacetime boom and some blacks found employment. In 1950, however, blacks still constituted a large percentage of the unemployed and underemployed work force. Consequently, civil rights organizations, especially the National Urban League, began to agitate for the strengthening and enforcement of the various laws which guaranteed equal employment opportunities. As early as 1945, President Truman recommended the establishment of a permanent Fair Employment Practice Commission (FEPC), but it wasn't until 1964 that fair employment legislation was enacted. The fair employment provisions of the Civil Rights Act of 1964: (1) prohibited persons from depriving others of equal employment opportunities on account of race, color, religion, sex, or national origin; (2) prohibited labor unions from refusing or limiting membership, discriminating in apprenticeships, or attempting to make an employer discriminate because of race, religion, sex, or national origin; and (3) established the Equal Employment Opportunities Commission with authority to resolve unlawful employment practices "through voluntary conciliation."

Since the issuance of Executive Orders 8802 (1941) and 9346 (1943) and the enactment of the Civil Rights Act of 1964, the number of blacks in the national work force has in fact increased. By 1970 firms with government contracts began to actively seek out and employ Afro-Americans. Most states had passed fair employment practice laws and labor unions had pledged to abolish racially segregated locals, to accept all eligible applicants for membership regardless of race, color, or creed, and to work for nondiscrimination provisions in all contracts made with management. The federal government continued its attack on the well-entrenched Jim Crow policies within its own agencies. Affirmative Action plans and Philadelphia Plans* have been adopted; union apprenticeship programs have been instituted; and goals and timetables have been established. However, some labor and management leaders argue that these schemes will prove unworkable and will lead to lower standards of excellence, reverse discrimination, and illegal quotas. Furthermore, although blacks have in fact gained easier access to the job market and are no longer hired "exclusively" at entry-level jobs, a disproportionately large number are locked into the bottom half of the employment pyramid.

Recently, blacks have won court decisions involving job discrimination. A federal court in February 1974 in Atlanta, Georgia, ordered the Georgia Power Company to pay almost $2.1 million to blacks who were victims of job discrimination. In other instances, agreements have been

*In which Government contractors pledge to hire a specified quota of minority employees.

reached between blacks and some industries with regard to unlawful employment practices. In April 1974, ten of the leading steel companies in the country agreed to pay more than 50,000 workers $30 million in back wages to compensate for past sex and racial bias in job discrimination. Taking advantage of various federal programs, especially those offered through the Office of Minority Business Enterprise of the Small Business Administration, Afro-Americans across the nation have attempted to become entrepeneurs. Some have secured franchises with national or regional businesses, while others have established independent businesses. In both cases, however, the black businessperson, in order to achieve some measure of economic success, must have continuous technical assistance and sufficient risk capital.

Blacks are still not being employed in the top management positions. A survey of the 50 largest corporations in the United States in October 1970 indicated that there were no blacks among their 2522 executives and only three blacks were among the 660 directors of these companies. And, although there have been dramatic increases in the number of Afro-Americans being employed in predominantly white institutions of higher learning and in federal and state jobs, it is rare to find black college or university presidents or vice presidents at predominantly white institutions or to find blacks in the "super grades" of the federal and state civil service.

Furthermore, despite all the efforts of recent years, the dollar gap that separates whites and blacks continues to grow. In 1950, the median white family income was $3,445 and the median black family income was $1,869—a dollar gap of $1,576. By 1967, amid widely heralded fair employment practice legislation, white family income soared to $8,318 and black income to $4,939. The dollar gap was then $3,379. A Bureau of Labor Statistics report, "The Social and Economic Status of the Black Population in the United States, 1973," pointed out that the median income for a black family of two adults and two children was $7,269, up from $6,864 in 1972. For a white family, however, it was $12,595, up from $11,549, resulting in a gap of $5,362.

Unemployment rates among blacks climbed during the civil rights years. In 1968 the federal government announced a national unemployment rate of 3.6 percent, the lowest in fifteen years. However, the announcement did not point out that in the same year the unemployment rate for blacks was 7 percent, that the unemployment rate in the black ghettos was 9 percent, that unemployment reached the disastrous rate of about one out of every four black teenagers, and that underemployment ranged up to one-half of all black workers. In 1972, the unemployment rate for blacks sixteen and over had increased to 10 percent, while that for whites was 5 percent.

EDUCATION

Until the post-World War II years very little had been accomplished with regard to equal educational opportunities for blacks. In 1954, however, the Supreme Court in *Brown* vs. *The Board of Education of Topeka, Kansas,* held that the doctrine of separate but equal had no place in public education and that separate educational facilities were "inherently" unequal.

The Brown decision was bitterly resented. Several anti-Supreme Court bills were introduced in Congress. Southern states established private all-white schools and closed public schools to prevent school integration. White Citizens Councils, organized in Mississippi in 1955, and the Ku Klux Clan used terrorist tactics to prevent integration of schools. In September 1957 Governor Orval E. Faubus ordered out the National Guard to prevent nine black students from attending all-white Central High School in Little Rock, Arkansas. In June 1963, Alabama Governor George C. Wallace carried out his compaign pledge and "stood in the schoolhouse door" to prevent integration of Alabama schools.

In the face of such defiance, which often resulted in rioting, extensive property damage, serious injuries, and death, the United States Supreme Court continued to hand down rulings favorable to school integration; the result was "some integration in primary and secondary schools in all 17 of the former Confederate states and the border states and the District of Columbia that provided for school segregation in their Constitution or by statute."

A provision of the Civil Rights Act of 1964 sought to further aid the school desegregation effort by authorizing the federal government to give technical and financial assistance to public school systems in the process of desegregation; it also authorized the U.S. Attorney General to file suit for the desegregation of public schools and colleges.

Desegregation of elementary and secondary schools in the South has had one devastating effect, i.e., the lay-off of many black teachers. In a statewide survey, sixteen South Carolina school districts showed a loss of 221 black teachers from 1967 to 1969, while the total number of white teachers increased by 366 during the same period. There were also many problems associated with the desegregation of institutions of higher learning in the South; demonstrations and riots erupted when black students attempted to gain admission to all-white institutions. In the fall of 1970, however, out of a total of 1,292,053 students there were 175,000 blacks (13 percent) attending predominantly white institutions of higher learning in the South.

In the North, East, and West during the early 1960s, blacks began to tire of their all-black, substandard ghetto schools and initiated a series of school boycotts protesting de facto segregation. The result was the adoption of various schemes to achieve some sort of racial balance in the schools. This, however, was not done without a white backlash. The announcement of a school integration plan in San Francisco, California, in 1973 caused a serious boycott of the schools by whites, the establishment of private schools, and strong protest from such groups as the National Socialist White People's Party (Nazi).

In June 1974 a federal judge ruled that the Boston School Committee had "intentionally segregated schools at all levels" and in effect ran a dual school system for its 36,000 nonwhite students. He ordered the bussing of 8,150 white students and 9,725 nonwhite students. In addition, 27,000 of the system's 94,000 students were assigned to new schools. The changes primarily affected Roxbury, center of Boston's black community, and South Boston, the white Irish Catholic stronghold. Implementation of the order when schools opened in September was followed by violent clashes, property damage, and injury to many persons; whites and blacks boycotted the schools; and demonstrations were held by neo-Nazis, the KKK, and the NAACP. Busses were stoned, shots were exchanged, fistfights broke out between students, and there were several stabbings and deaths.

In October, the judge ordered the all-white Boston School Committee to draw up and approve a new integration plan by December 1974. The committee defied the deadline, rejecting the new plan 3 to 2, but the Committee's attorney turned the three-hundred-page report over to the Court. The new plan called for bussing about 35,000 students in all parts of the city.

An Appellate Court, in a unanimous decision, upheld the lower court's ruling that required desegregation of Boston's schools, while acknowledging that racial tensions and violence had marred Boston school integration; the court added that "while Boston is unique in some of its traditions, demographic profile and style, its uniqueness cannot exempt it from complying with a national policy forged long ago and laboriously implemented throughout the land."

In the predominantly white institutions of higher learning in the North,

East, and West, efforts to admit black students did not get under way until the 1960s and especially after the assassination of the Rev. Dr. Martin Luther King, Jr., in 1968. Special programs, generally called educational opportunity programs, were established whereby blacks, who would otherwise be inadmissible because of low grade point averages and test scores, would be "specially" admitted and provided with the necessary "supportive services" (tutoring, counseling, financial aid, etc.) to aid them in the pursuit of their degrees. The consequence of this effort has been a tremendous increase in black students.

Associated with the increase of black students in predominantly white institutions of higher learning has been the establishment of departments of black studies. Although such programs were instituted on a very large scale in the late 1960s, cutbacks in budgets and student financial aid, as well as increased criticism of the academic value of black studies, have seriously endangered such programs.

The efforts to increase the number of black students on predominantly white campuses have not gone unchallenged. In 1971, Marco DeFunis, a white student at the University of Washington, filed suit claiming that he was denied a place in law school while several less qualified blacks were admitted under the special minority admissions program. He alleged that he was barred on account of race and therefore was denied his civil rights. The lower court agreed with DeFunis but an appeals court ruled for the University. Because DeFunis had finished law school, the U.S. Supreme Court ruled that the case was moot and thereby inferentially at least upheld the appeals court. In 1974 the San Francisco Office of the Department of Health, Education, and Welfare received a complaint from the Anti-Defamation League of B'nai B'rith on behalf of itself and five other national Jewish organizations alleging "reverse discrimination" and "preferential treatment" in the admission of minority students into the Berkeley campus of the University of California.

With the requirement to dismantle the dual system of higher education in the South, it seems clear that predominantly black institutions of higher learning will also have to refrain from discrimination in administration and to begin faculty desegregation. As a result, many black educators fear that desegregation will transform the black institutions into predominantly white institutions which will basically serve the needs of whites. They argue that black institutions of higher learning should be allowed to retain their distinctive identity although allowing admissions on a nondiscriminatory basis, and further that "such institutions be given both adequate budgets and the primary responsibility for those aspects of education of particular interest to the black community, such as social welfare, community planning, and community health."*

HOUSING

Despite some economic gains made during and after World War II, Afro-Americans found it very difficult to live in communities of their choice. Although discriminatory restrictions on the right of occupancy had been declared unconstitutional and unenforceable, segregation in the sale and rental of houses had become a permanent part of the American way of life.

In an effort to break down racial segregation in housing, civil rights groups called for legislation guaranteeing the sale or rental of houses without regard to race, creed, or color. The result was the issuance of Executive Order 11063 in 1962 prohibiting discrimination in the sale or rental of some federally financed housing. In addition, the Fair Housing Act of 1968 extended this prohibition to cover the sale or rental of 80 percent of all housing, including single-family residences.

States and municipalities were also acting. By early 1963, eighteen states and fifty-five cities had passed "open occupancy" laws which prevented discrimination in the sale, purchase, or rental of real property, provided for conciliation where there were disputes, and sometimes established penalties in cases where discrimination was found.

In spite of federal, state, and municipal legislation, complaints of discrimination against blacks in the purchase or rental of real property continues to mount. In June 1973 a report of the San Francisco Human Relations Commission set forth twelve typical cases of racial discrimination, including an out-of-court settlement of $1500 that was paid by a white landlord who had asked a white woman to move out because she entertained black guests.

PUBLIC ACCOMMODATIONS

Under the doctrine of separate but equal, blacks were segregated or discriminated against in places of public accommodations. Where there were

*"The Future of the Black Colleges," *Daedalus*, Summer 1971.

no laws providing for segregation and discrimination such a practice evolved, resulting in de facto segregation and discrimination. Imbued with a sense of democracy by their fight "to make the world safe for democracy," and impatient with the NAACP's methods of achieving equal rights by court action, blacks in the South initiated the Montgomery Bus Boycott in 1955, began sit-ins in 1960, and launched the freedom rides in 1961.

White Southerners were determined to preserve the status quo—separate and ostensibly equal. Confronted on the one hand by the Ku Klux Klan and White Citizens Councils, Afro-Americans in the South were also threatened with economic reprisals; they were stoned, bombed, and harassed; and their property was destroyed.

Congress responded with the passage of the Civil Rights Act of 1964 which prohibited discrimination because of race, religion, color, or national origin in places of public accommodation and permitted persons who were denied their rights to sue civilly for damages. Furthermore, the 1968 amendment to the Civil Rights Act of 1964 made it a criminal offense to injure or intimidate a person because that person used or urged others to use public accommodations.

EQUAL PROTECTION OF THE LAWS

Prior to the civil rights years, Afro-Americans had been denied equal protection of the laws as guaranteed by the 14th Amendment. Black civil rights demonstrators historically suffered injury and death at the hands of white segregationists.

During the civil rights years, blacks throughout the nation grew more and more frustrated by having to live in ghettos, by their inability to find jobs, by decaying schools, by lack of trust in the police, and by de facto and de jure segregation in places of public accommodation. Feeling both a growing sense of power and a deepening sense of frustration, they became patently angered by the fact that for centuries blacks had been robbed of their civil rights, property, families, dignity, history, and lives. Black sit-inners, freedom riders, boycotters, and picketers increased their efforts to secure equal protection of the laws. The urgency of their efforts was best evidenced in August 1963 when over 200,000 Americans of all creeds and colors, led by Rev. Dr. Martin Luther King, Jr., gathered in Washington, D.C., and demanded that the United States Government immediately address itself to the unfinished task of freedom and justice for all. Rev. King stated ". . . that one day this nation will rise up and live out the true meaning of its creed: We hold these truths to be self-evident, that all men are created equal . . . ."

Although in 1948 President Truman had asked Congress to pass legislation that would provide protection for blacks against deprivation of their civil rights, it was not until 1964 that Congress acted. A provision was included in the Civil Rights Act of 1964 authorizing the U.S. Attorney General to intervene in private suits in which there was alleged a denial of equal protection of the laws and when the case was of "general public importance." In addition, the 1968 amendment to the Civil Rights Act of 1964 further guaranteed blacks equal protection of the laws by prohibiting the injuring or intimidating of any person because that person was voting or compaigning for office, serving on a federal jury, or working for a federal agency or participating in a federal or federally assisted program; it also prohibited interference with a person because of race while that person was attending a public school or college, participating in a state or locally administered program, working for a state, local, or private employer, or joining a labor union.

DEMONSTRATION AND RIOTS

Although Congress enacted several major civil rights bills between 1957 and 1968, this legislation usually came in the wake of large civil demonstrations. Cities in most parts of the nation experienced demonstrations of some type and most urban centers with large black populations experienced riots and substantial violence. There were more than twenty major riots between the time of the Montgomery Bus Boycott, which began on December 5, 1955, and the Detroit riots of July 23-28, 1967, during which more than 4000 fires were set, extensive sniping occurred, forty-three persons died, and at least 657 were injured.

During this same period (1955-1967) the nation was not unaware of its racial problems. In 1946 President Truman appointed a Committee on Civil Rights to advise him on the condition of blacks. The Civil Rights Commission, established in 1957, had issued four major reports by 1965. In March 1965, the Department of Labor's Office of Policy Planning and Research issued the controversial report, "The Negro Family: The Case for National Planning" (The Moynihan Report). In June 1966 the White House Conference, "To Fulfil These Rights," was sponsored by President Lyndon B. Johnson and in 1967 President Johnson appointed the National

Commission on Civil Disorder which issued a blistering report in March 1968.

All of these bodies pointed out the nature of the race problems, i.e., discriminatory police practices; unemployment and underemployment; inadequate housing, education, welfare programs, and municipal services; poor recreational facilities and programs; and discriminatory consumer and credit practices. The National Advisory Commission on Civil Disorders categorically stated that "white racism, which had permeated much of American life [w]as the deep, underlying cause of urban unrest." It also pointed out that it found no evidence that any of the riots were the result of "any organized plan or conspiracy" as alleged by J. Edgar Hoover, Director of the Federal Bureau of Investigation.

ARMED SERVICES

Yielding to pressure to end segregation and discrimination in the armed services in 1948, President Truman issued Executive Order 9981, banning segregation in the military. In the years since there continued to be racial clashes between black and white United States troops, both at home and abroad.

In October 1972 there was a major race riot aboard the USS *Kitty Hawk*. Of the twenty-eight black sailors who were charged with various offenses (and who were held in jail 65 days before being brought to trial) nineteen were found guilty, while the one white sailor who had been charged was acquitted early in the proceedings. On January 2, 1973, an all-white Congressional subcommittee was appointed to investigate the matter. The subcommittee found that the riot was due to "permissiveness" and not racial discrimination, a conclusion reached without talking to any of the two hundred black sailors involved in the incident.

The *Kitty Hawk* riot was a dramatic incident, but both the Korean War and the Vietnam War were continuously marked by black-white racial clashes. In a report to Congress in July 1970 about racial tensions in the Vietnam War, black Congressman Augustus F. Hawkins stated that "racial bias, unequal assignments, double standards and lack of understanding at the command level" have resulted in a "fighting force whose minority members are unequally treated by a predominantly white chain of command." Other reasons cited for racial strife in the armed services were that many blacks received nonjudicial punishment disproportionate to their numbers in the military; that in 1973 approximately 36 percent of all

American soldiers in stockades worldwide were black; that a large percentage of servicemen in veterans hospitals suffering psychological disturbances were black; and that black troops incur a disproportionately large percentage of casualties and fatalities in war.

Black servicemen and women in the civil rights years and after increasingly adopted the trappings and rhetoric of black militants. Quite often this black militance took organizational form such as the Moormen at Quantico Marine Base in Virginia, the Modern Minority Officers at Fort Benning, Georgia, the Concerned Veterans of Vietnam, and the Black Serviceman's Caucus at San Diego, California. These and other organizations were formed to insure equal treatment of blacks in the armed services, for black servicemen and women realized that racism was institutionalized at all levels of the military and nothing appeared to be changing.

SPORTS

In responding to the demand to recruit and admit black students, many predominantly white institutions of higher learning recruited a large number of black athletes. With very rare exceptions, college and university coaches, who were always white, expected the black "recruits" to concentrate on the "job" for which they were "hired." Their primary goal was to maintain the black athletes' eligibility to play—not to educate black athletes. With the end of their eligibility, the black athletes found themselves in the academic arena without the aid of tutors and counselors who had previously written their term papers, taken their examinations, and planned their course of "academic study."

As the civil rights movement approached its zenith the revolt of the black athletes unfolded. Black athletes began to articulate their displeasure with racist coaching staffs, discriminatory practices of athletic departments, and the lack of meaningful social and cultural life on the campus and on road trips.

In reaction to such treatment, black athletes went on strike, refused to play against certain teams, and otherwise protested. Dr. Harry Edwards, black associate professor of sociology at the University of California, Berkeley, who attended San José State University on an athletic scholarship, continuously urged black athletes to boycott the Olympics and to rise up against the racist policies and practices which pervade college and university sports.

Although most athletic directors, who are generally white, hold the view that black athletes should not complain because sports has been good for them, some concessions have been made. Blacks have been hired on the coaching staffs, some effort has been made to insure that black athletes graduate "on time," and athletic committees have been established to investigate and settle cases of racial discrimination.

The racial problems that plague the black college and university athlete at predominantly white institutions also plague the black professional athlete. Although a few black superstars receive substantial salaries, in general black and white athletes of similar abilities are paid different salaries and few black athletes are given the opportunity to triple their salaries by endorsing commercial products or going on the lecture circuit.

There allegedly has been a behind-the-scenes drive to appoint blacks to executive and managerial positions. Black superstars in all major sports have earned the opportunity to manage and hold "front office" jobs.*

Hopefully, the racial impediments which continue to hinder black athletes in the university, college, and professional ranks, will be overcome more rapidly than they have in the past for, in the words of Harry Edwards "since 1968 the countless rebellions, boycotts and strikes carried out by black athletes and others have made it quite clear that the revolt in sports is a good deal more than a passing fad or political gesture."

SUPREME COURT DECISIONS

Prodded by the NAACP and the NAACP Legal Defense and Education Fund, the United States Supreme Court during the post–World War II years played a major role in improving the social, economic, and political status of Afro-Americans in the United States.

Beginning in 1938, the U.S. Supreme Court began to look at the concept of equality as it pertained to education. In *Missouri ex rel Gaines* vs. *Canada* (1938) the Court held that Missouri could not exclude a black from its state university law school when the only alternative offered was paid attendance at an out-of-state law school. Eleven years later in *Sweatt* vs. *Painter* (1949) the Court decreed that the "separate but equal doctrine" had not been satisfied and ordered Texas to admit a black to the all-white law school. In 1950 in *McLaurin* vs. *Oklahoma State Regents* the Court

*On October 3, 1974, Frank Robinson was named playing manager of the Cleveland Indians. Prior to this time professional basketball had several black head coaches.

stated that having admitted a black student, the University could not require him to eat, study, and sit in separate classrooms and eating places because such denied the student a fair opportunity to study, converse, and exchange views with other students. On May 17, 1954, the Court handed down the momentous *Brown* vs. *Board of Education of Topeka, Kansas*, decision.

Because of the demonstrations, boycotts, and sit-ins, which were led primarily by the members of the Congress of Racial Equality (CORE), Student Non-violent Coordinating Committee (SNCC), and the Council of Federated Organization (COFO), the Supreme Court became very involved in picketing and sit-ins. In a series of cases the Court held that Title II of the 1964 Civil Rights Act, barring discrimination in public accommodations, was constitutional; that peaceful civil rights demonstrations, even those inside public buildings, were protected by the First and Fourteenth Amendments; and that a person who violated another person's civil rights could be prosecuted both civilly and criminally.

BLACK NATIONALISM AND BLACK POWER

Expressions of black nationalism in one form or another have been heard in the United States since its founding. They become especially evident, however, in times of racial strife, frustration, and discord. After the Revolutionary War and the Reconstruction Era, when the ideals for which the wars were fought were not made applicable to blacks, blacks began to develop their own social, civil, educational, and cultural organizations, while at the same time demanding the rights guaranteed by the Constitution. Those blacks who became totally disillusioned and believed that blacks and whites could not live peaceably in the United States advocated emigration and colonization.

Since the decline of Garveyism in the 1920s, the most prominent black nationalist organization has been the Nation of Islam or the Black Muslims. Founded in the 1930s, the Black Muslims peaked in strength and influence during the civil rights years. Under the leadership of Malcolm X, the movement appealed to black ex-convicts and the black urban poor whose rights were largely unaffected by the civil rights movement. "Preaching the foreordained destruction of the white people" and its "replacement by a dominant black nation" the Black Muslims offered a "spiritual and psychological basis for black pride and a promise of future black supremacy . . . ."

After changing his philosophy with regard to the relationship between blacks and whites, Malcolm X divorced himself from the Black Muslims and founded another organization in 1964, but because he was assassinated in 1965 he did not have the opportunity to implement his new philosophy —peace and cooperation with whites.

In 1966, however, "black power" became the rallying cry of young blacks throughout the United States. Stokely Carmichael and Floyd McKissick shouted that the civil rights movement was doomed to failure because it was developed and directed by whites and that it was essential for blacks "to develop a strong political and economic power base within the black community . . . in order that they may control their own destinies." To them, black power meant black control of the institutions which directly affected the lives of blacks, especially those blacks in the inner cities.

Because black power rhetoric oftentimes carried with it overtones of "reverse racism" and separatism, the concept was initially rejected by the black advocates of integration. As the drive for equality became all-encompassing, with very few exceptions, black organizations of varying philosophies and ideologies came together in an effort to achieve "first class citizenship."

REFERENCES

Bell, Carolyn Shaw, *The Economics of the Ghetto* (New York: Pegasus, 1970).

Bell, Howard H., ed., *Black Separatism and the Caribbean* (Ann Arbor: University of Michigan Press, 1970).

——, *Search for a Place: Black Separatism and Africa* (Ann Arbor: University of Michigan Press, 1969).

Benedict, Stewart H., ed., *Blacklash* (New York: Popular Library, 1970).

Berry, Mary F., *Black Resistance/White Law* (New York: Appleton Press, 1971).

"The Black Athlete," *The Black Scholar*, III (Nov. 1971).

"The Black Athlete—A Shameful Story," *Sports Illustrated*, XXIX (July 1, 1968, pp. 12-27; July 8, 1968, pp. 18-31; July 15, 1968, pp. 28-43; July 22, 1968, pp. 28-41; July 29, 1968, pp. 20-35).

"The Black Soldier," *The Black Scholar*, II (Nov. 1970).

"Black Soldier, II," *The Black Scholar*, V (Oct. 1973).

Black Sports (Published monthly by Black Sports, Inc., New York).

Blauner, Robert, *Racial Oppression in America* (New York: Harper and Row, 1973).

Blaustein, Albert, and Robert Zandrando, eds., *Civil Rights and the American Negro* (New York: Trident Press, 1968).

Carmichael, Stokely, *Stokely Speaks* (New York: Vintage Books, 1971).

Davidson, Chandler, *Biracial Politics: Conflict and Coalition in the Metropolitan South* (Baton Rouge: Louisiana State University Press, 1972).

Draper, Theodore, *The Discovery of Black Nationalism* (New York: Viking Press, 1970).

Edwards, Harry, *Up Toward Liberation* (New York: The Free Press, 1970).

——, *The Revolt of the Black Athlete* (New York: The Free Press, 1969).

Essien-Udom, E., *Black Nationalism: The Search for Identity in America* (Chicago: University of Chicago Press, 1962).

Ginger, Ann Fagan, *The Law, the Supreme Court, and the People's Rights* (New York: Barron's Educational Series, Inc., 1973).

Griggs, Anthony, "Minorities in the Armed Services," *Race Relations Reporter*, IV (July 1973, pp. 9-14, and Sept. 1973, pp. 26-29).

Haskins, Jim, ed., *Black Manifesto for Education* (New York: William Morrow and Co., Inc., 1973).

Jordan, Winthrop D., *The White Man's Burden* (New York: Oxford University Press, 1974).

Lecky, Robert S., and H. Elliot Wright, eds., *Black Manifesto: Religion, Racism, and Reparations* (New York: Sheed and Ward, 1969).

Lincoln, C. Eric, *The Black Muslims in America* (Boston: Beacon Press, 1961).

Littleton, Arthur L., and Mary W. Burger, *Black Viewpoints* (New York: New American Library, 1971).

Lomax, Louis E., *When the Word is Given: A Report on Elijah Muhammad, Malcolm X, and the Black Muslim World* (Cleveland: World Pubishers, 1963).

Lynch, Hollis R., *The Black Urban Condition* (New York: Thomas Crowell Co., 1973).

——, *Edward Wilmot Blyden, Pan-Negro Patriot 1832-1912* (London: Oxford University Press, 1970).

Mack, Raymond W., ed., *Our Children's Burden: Studies of Desegregation in Nine American Communities* (New York: Random House, 1968).

Matthews, Vincent, *My Race Be Won* (New York: Charterhouse, 1974).

McEvoy, James, and Abraham Miller, eds., *Black Power and Student Rebellion* (Belmont: Wadsworth Publishing Co., Inc., 1969).

Meier, August, *Negro Thought in America, 1880-1915* (Ann Arbor: University of Michigan Press, 1963).

_____, Elliott Rudwick, and John H. Bracey, Jr., eds., *Black Nationalism in America* (New York: Bobbs-Merrill Co., Inc., 1970).

_____, _____, and Francis L. Broderick, eds., *Black Protest Thought in the Twentieth Century*, 2nd ed. (New York: Bobbs-Merrill Co., Inc., 1971).

Muhammad, Elijah, *Message to the Black Man in America* (Chicago: Muhammad Mosque of Islam, 1965).

Mullen, Robert W., *Blacks in American Wars* (New York: Monad Press, 1973).

Muse, Benjamin, *The American Negro Revolution: From Nonviolence to Black Power, 1963-1967* (Bloomington: Indiana University Press, 1968).

Nelson, Jack, and Jack Bass, *The Orangeburg Massacre* (New York: Ballantine Books, 1970).

Newton, Huey P., *Revolutionary Suicide* (New York: Harcourt Brace Jovanovich, 1973).

_____, *To Die for the People* (New York: Vintage Books, 1972).

Pease, William H., and Jane H. Pease, *Black Utopia: Negro Communal Experiments in America* (Madison: State Historic Society of Wisconsin, 1963).

Pugh, Douglas, ed., *Black Economic Development* (New York: Prentice-Hall, Inc., 1969).

Redkey, Edwin S., *Black Exodus: Black Nationalist and Back-to-Africa Movements, 1890-1910* (New Haven: Yale University Press, 1969).

Report of the National Advisory Commission on Civil Disorders (Washington, D.C.: Government Printing Office, 1968).

Report of the Task Force on the Administration of Military Justice in the Armed Services, 4 vols. (Washington, D.C.: Government Printing Office, 1972).

Smith, Baxter, *FBI Plot Against the Black Movement* (New York: Pathfinder Press Inc., 1972).

Tabb, William K., *The Political Economy of the Black Ghetto* (New York: W. W. Norton and Co., 1970).

Taylor, Clyde, ed., *Vietnam and Black America: An Anthology of Protest and Resistance* (New York: Doubleday, 1973).

Thibodeaux, Mary Roger, *A Black Nun Looks at Black Power* (New York: Sheed and Ward, 1972).

Ullman, Victor, *Martin R. Delaney: The Beginnings of Black Nationalism* (Boston: Beacon Press, 1971).

Vatter, Harold G., and Thomas Palm, *The Economics of Black America* (New York: Harcourt Brace Jovanovich, 1972).

Walton, Hanes, Jr., *Black Political Parties: An Historical and Political Analysis* (New York: The Free Press, 1972).

——, *Black Politics: A Theoretical and Structural Analysis* (Philadelphia: J. B. Lippincott, 1972).

——, *The Negro in Third Party Politics* (Philadelphia: Dorrance & Co., 1969).

——, *The Political Philosophy of Martin Luther King Jr.* (Westport: Negro University Press, 1971).

Wright, Nathan, Jr., *What Black Educators Are Saying* (New York: Hawthorn Books Inc., 1970).

31
The Nixon Years

Presidents Truman, Eisenhower, Kennedy, and Johnson had initiated and actively supported legislation that would insure equal rights for blacks, but President Richard M. Nixon instituted a policy of "benign neglect" (the race issue would resolve itself if left alone). This change in policy resulted from a confidential memo written by Presidential Counsellor Patrick Moynihan, which completely contradicted the analysis in Moynihan's *The Negro Family: The Case for National Action* "for carrying out the complex task of bringing Negro Americans into full participation in the society" (issued in March 1965 when Moynihan was Assistant Secretary of Labor and Director of the Office of Policy Planning and Research of the Department of Labor).

Summarizing the attitude of blacks, Carl Rowan, a former diplomat and noted newspaper columnist, stated "Black America has been in limbo for all the Nixon years, with no real hope of major new progress toward first-class citizenship. They have struggled mostly to prevent an Administration they regarded as hostile from erasing or eroding the fragile freedom gained in a generation of protesting, suing, bleeding, dying. . . ."

As the federal courts began to hand down school desegregation decisions attacking school segregation in states outside the South, legislators began to raise their voices in opposition, especially against bussing as a means of integrating the schools. In November 1971, an amendment to an education desegregation aid bill would have "postponed . . . the effective date of any court order requiring bussing, forbade the use of all federal education funds for bussing to overcome racial imbalance and forbade federal pressure on local school agencies to spend state or local funds for bussing."

On May 17, 1974, the twentieth anniversary of the landmark school desegregation case *Brown* vs. *Board of Education of Topeka, Kansas,* a $200 million class action suit was filed in a Topeka court charging the local school board with failure to fully integrate the school system and with favoritism in providing better facilities and better qualified staff members for the white schools.

In the area of housing, Nixon in June 1971 stated that the administration would oppose segregation in housing based on race, but would not interfere with local zoning laws whose effect was to exclude some persons for economic reasons. The consequence of such policy was the sanctioning of zoning laws which effectively prohibited blacks from renting or buying houses in the suburbs to which white families and business and industry are fleeing. Despite Nixon's statement however, the federal government in 1971 sued the St. Louis suburb of Black Jack when it was pointed out that the land had been rezoned specifically to prohibit construction of a middle income housing project which would attract blacks.

The Philadelphia Plan, which by late 1972 had been adopted by New York, Los Angeles, San Francisco, Seattle, and approximately fifty other cities, came under attack. Contending the plan violated the Civil Rights Act of 1964, the AFL-CIO vigorously opposed the plan and it barely survived a move in Congress to terminate it, even though the Civil Rights Commission issued a report in May 1969, *Jobs and Civil Rights,* which accused the federal government of using public funds to subsidize employment discrimination and called for the enactment of Executive Order 10925, which forbade job discrimination by federal contractors.

Nixon's plans to dismantle the Office of Economic Opportunity, "the nerve center of the war on poverty," brought cries of 'shame' and 'inhumane' from the black population.

Reacting to the fact that the civil rights movement had clearly reached its low point with Nixon's election, and failing to obtain a meeting with the President to discuss civil rights issues, black members of the House of Representatives, on October 14, 1970, announced that they were forming a "shadow cabinet" to monitor federal enforcement of the civil rights laws. Six months later, on March 25, 1971, Nixon met with the black congressmen who urged him to "unequivocally" set as a national goal the equality of all citizens and recommended 60 actions that he might take to demonstrate his commitment to equality. In May, in a reply characterized by the black Representatives as "deeply disappointing," Nixon indicated that his administration shared the goal of equality. Stating that the Nixon administration "by word and deed, was retreating at crucial points from the national commitment to equality," the 'shadow cabinet' organized itself as the Congressional Black Caucus. The thirteen members of the Caucus stated that they were "congressmen-at-large, representing all black citizens of the United States" and they pledged themselves to monitor federal enforcement of civil rights laws and expose any federal official who was guilty of being lax in the enforcement of such laws.

However, since 1969, civil rights has not suffered from total "benign neglect." In August 1969, Nixon issued Executive Order 11478 which ordered federal department heads to develop "affirmative programs" to eliminate job discrimination in government agencies and authorized the Civil Service Commission to oversee each Department's program and resolve complaints of job discrimination.

In 1970, the Voting Rights Act of 1965, under which almost one million black citizens in the South registered to vote, was extended for five more years, despite the opposition of the Nixon Administration.

In March 1971, Congress approved the Twenty-sixth Amendment, lowering the voting age for federal, state, and local elections; within a few months, the necessary number of states had ratified it. Approximately 11 million young people, a good many of them black, were made eligible to vote in the 1972 elections and thereafter.

In 1972, legislation was enacted which gave the Equal Employment Opportunity Commission (EEOC) the power to enforce its findings of job discrimination. This legislation remedied a deficiency in the 1964 Act which created a "conciliatory" EEOC without enforcement powers.

During the Nixon years the Supreme Court continued to hand down favorable civil rights decisions. In *Sullivan* vs. *Little Hunting Park Inc.* (1969) the Court interpreted the Civil Rights Act of 1866 to prohibit a community swim club from denying membership to a black man leasing a home in the community served by the swim club. In *Swann* vs. *Charlotte-Meckenburg County Board* (1971), the Court approved the use of bussing, racial balance ratios, and gerrymandered school districts as interim means of desegregating schools. In *Oregon* vs. *Mitchell* (1970) the Court approved congressional action to lower the voting age for federal elections, to restrict state residence requirements for voting in presidential elections, and to ban literacy tests—but disapproved legislation approved by Congress to lower the voting age for state and local elections. In *Griggs* vs. *Duke Power Co.*

(1971) the Court held that the Civil Rights Act prohibited an employer from requiring a high-school diploma or general score on an intelligence test as a condition for employment or promotion if the test was not related to job skills and if it tended to disqualify more black than white applicants.

However, in a decision that shocked civil rights leaders (*Millikan* vs. *Bradley*, 1974) the Court held that Detroit, with its predominantly black school system, need not engage in a metropolitan bussing program to mix the city's students with students from the predominantly white schools in 53 surrounding suburbs.

The past fifteen years have seen significant changes in the civil rights movement. When the movement began in the early 1960s, only the judiciary had been actively engaged in attempting to protect the constitutional rights of black people. Even though executive orders during the 1940s and 1950s had desegregated the armed services and attacked discrimination in employment and the Civil Rights Bill of 1957 had been enacted, the executive and legislative branches had not actively asserted themselves. But during the 1960s, for the first time in the history of our nation all three branches of government became intensively involved in the civil rights struggle, resulting in a host of federal laws and policies designed to guarantee blacks equal protection of the law.

Now it has become very clear that these laws and policies attack only one aspect of the civil rights problem—legal inequalities—and it is equally clear that what is needed now is a policy which tackles "those aspects of civil rights that involve social and economic aspects of the Negro's position in American society." In all of the areas in which civil rights laws afford legal protection—education, housing, employment, voting, and public accommodations—discrimination persists. The bases for this persistence are the "social and economic injustices which have been allowed to grow and ferment for many years." Hopefully the next decade will bring about "equal protection of the law" for *all* Americans.

REFERENCES

"Blacks and the Law," *The Annals*, CDVII (May 1973).

Campbell, Angus, *White Attitudes Toward Black People* (Ann Arbor: University of Michigan Press, 1971).

Federal Civil Rights Enforcement Effort (Washington, D.C.: Government Printing Office, 1971).

Henderson, Lenneal J., Jr., ed., *Black Political Life in the United States* (San Francisco: Chandler Publishing Co., 1972).

Moynihan, Daniel P., *The Negro Family: The Case for National Action* (Washington, D.C.: Office of Policy Planning and Research, U.S. Department of Labor, 1965).

Murphy, Reg, and Hal Gulliver, *The Southern Strategy* (New York: Charles Scribner's Sons, 1971).

Rainwater, Lee, *Behind Ghetto Walls* (Chicago: Aldine Publishing Co., 1970).

_____, and William Yancey, eds., *The Moynihan Report and the Politics of Controversy* (Cambridge: MIT Press, 1967).

Rowan, Carl T., *Just Between Us Blacks* (New York: Random House, 1974).

Schuman, Howard, and Shirley Hatchett, *Black Racial Attitudes, Trends and Complexities* (Ann Arbor: University of Michigan Press, 1974).

Urban America, Inc., and The Urban Coalition, *One Year Later* (New York: Frederick A. Praeger Publishers, 1969).

General References

Aptheker, Herbert C., *Afro-American History: The Modern Era* (New York: Citadel Press, 1971).

*_____, ed., *A Documentary History of the Negro in the United States*, 2 Vols. (New York: Citadel Press, 1964 [Citadel]).

*Bennett, Lerone, Jr., *Before the Mayflower: A History of the Negro in America, 1619–1962* (Chicago: Johnson Publishing Co., 1964 [Penguin]).

Brown, Ina C., *The Story of the American Negro* (New York: Friendship Press, 1957).

A CBS New Reference Book: Civil Rights (New York: R. R. Bowker Co., 1974).

Chase, William M., and Peter Collier, eds., *Justice Denied: The Blackman in White America* (New York: Harcourt Brace Jovanovich, Inc., 1970).

Fishel, Leslie H., Jr., and Benjamin Quarles, eds., *The Black American: A Documentary History*, 3rd ed. (Glenview: Scott, Foresman and Company, 1976).

Davie, Maurice, *Negroes in American Society* (New York: McGraw-Hill, 1949).

Davis, John P., ed., *The American Negro Reference Book* (Englewood Cliffs, N.J.: Prentice-Hall, 1966).

Franklin, John Hope, *From Slavery to Freedom: A History of American Negroes* (New York: Alfred A. Knopf, 1967).

Frazier, E. Franklin, *The Negro in the United States* (Chicago: The University of Chicago Press, 1966).

Harris, Middleton; Morris Levitt; Roger Furman; and Ernest Smith, eds., *The Black Book* (New York: Random House, 1974).

*Logan, Rayford W., *The Negro in the United States: A Brief Review* (Princeton, N. J.: J. D. Van Nostrand Co., 1957 [Anvil]).

Meier, August, and Francis L. Broderick, *From Plantation to Ghetto* (New York: Hill & Wang, 1966).

*Meltzer, Milton, *In Their Own Words: A History of the American Negro*, 3 Vols. (New York: Apollo Editions, Vol. 1, 1964; Vol. 2, 1965; Vol. 3, 1967).

Mergman, Peter M., *The Chronological History of the Negro in America* (New York: Harper & Row, 1969).

The Negro in American History (Chicago: Encyclopaedia Britannica, 1970).

*Quarles, Benjamin, *The Negro in the Making of America* (New York: Collier, Macmillan, 1964 [Collier, Macmillan]).

Sloan, Irving J., *The American Negro: A Chronology and Fact Book* (Dobbs Ferry, N.Y.: Oceana Publications, 1965).

Wade, Richard, *The Negro in American Life, Selected Readings* (New York: Houghton, Mifflin, 1965).

Williams, George Washington, *History of the Negro Race in America, From 1619 to 1880* (New York: G. P. Putnam's Sons, 1883).

Woodson, Carter G., *The Negro in Our History*, 10th rev. ed. (Washington, D.C.: Associated Publishers, Inc., 1959).

Chronological Table of Events

4	Ghana Empire founded
1230	Empire of Mali founded
1434	Portuguese began exploration of West African coast and engaged in trade on a small scale
1441	Portuguese Slave Trade began
1464	Emergence of the Songhay Empire
1501	Spanish decree sanctioned the introduction of black slaves into Spanish colonies in the New World
1517	Bishop Las Casas received permission to allow each Spanish immigrant family to the New World to bring 12 black slaves
1550	Trading agreements made between Europeans and African coastal kingdoms
1619	Twenty blacks landed at Jamestown, Va.
1660	Beginning of the Ashanti Empire

1670	Institution of slavery legally recognized in all colonies
1688	Mennonite Quakers of Germantown, Pa., denounce slavery
1700	New England shippers began to import slaves directly from Africa
1712	First major slave insurrection in North American colonies in New York City
1720– 1739	Serious slave revolts in South Carolina, Virginia, Louisiana
1723	Crispus Attacks shot to death at the Boston Massacre
1773– 1799	Petitions for freedom by Boston Afro-Americans
1775	Exclusion of black soldiers in the Continental Army
	First emancipation society formed in Philadelphia
1776	Continental Congress approved enlistment of free blacks
1777– 1827	Vermont was first state to abolish slavery; Pennsylvania in 1780 (gradually); Massachusetts and New Hampshire in 1783; Connecticut and Rhode Island in 1784; New York 1827 (gradually); and New Jersey in 1804
1783	Peace of Paris, ending the Revolutionary War, provided for the return of slaves captured by the British
1786	Importation of slaves ended in all states but South Carolina and Georgia
1787	Continental Congress excluded slavery from the Northwest Territory
1790	All states ratified the United States Constitution, containing provisions for the return of fugitive slaves, counting slaves as three-fifths of a person for purposes of taxation and representation, and sanctioning the slave trade until 1808

1791	The Bill of Rights, first ten amendments to the Constitution
1793	Fugitive Slave Act passed
	Cotton gin invented
1802	Successful uprising in Santo Domingo led by Touissant L'Ouverture
1807	British impressed four American seamen, three blacks and one white, from U.S.S. *Chesapeake*—a major cause of the War of 1812
	Great Britain abolished slave trade
1808	Federal law banning African slave trade
1815	Two regiments of free blacks fought under General Jackson in the Battle of New Orleans
1816	American Colonization Society organized to transport free blacks to Africa
1818	Andrew Jackson defeated force of Indians and blacks at Battle of Suwanee, ending the First Seminole War
1820	Missouri Compromise: Maine admitted as free state, Missouri as slave state, and slavery prohibited in the Louisiana Purchase north of 36–30 latitude
1827	First black newspaper, *Freedom's Journal*, published in New York City
1829	David Walker's "Appeal," calling for blacks to openly revolt, published
	Robert Alexander Young, a free black, published *The Ethiopian Manifesto*
	Mexico abolished slavery
1830	Indian Removal Act, called for moving Indians (Sauk, Fox, Choctaw, Chickasaw, Cherokee, and Seminoles) westward across the Mississippi River, making way for the Cotton Kingdom

1831   William Lloyd Garrison's *Liberator* began publication

Nat Turner led nation's largest slave revolt in Southampton County, Va.

1833   American Anti-Slavery Society organized in Philadelphia

1834   Slavery abolished in the British Empire

Slavery prohibited in Jamaica

1836   "The Gag Rule" passed by the House, providing for the laying aside of all antislavery petitions to the House. The House adopted a stricter "gag rule" every year until 1844

1838   Calhoun's Resolutions, stating that Congress was not to interfere with slavery in the states, the District of Columbia, or the territories, passed in the Senate

1840   American and Foreign Antislavery Society founded

House voted to not even receive antislavery petitions

1842   *Prigg* vs. *Pennsylvania:* Supreme Court ruled that states had no power over cases arising under the Fugitive Slave Act, thus preventing states from either helping or hindering fugitive slaves

1845   Texas admitted to the Union with slavery

1846   Representative David Wilmot proposed the exclusion of slavery from territory acquired from Mexico as a result of the Mexican War

1848   Bill introduced to extend to Oregon the Northwest Territory restrictions on slavery. Another amendment was introduced to extend the Missouri Compromise line to the Pacific Ocean, thus extending slavery into New Mexico and parts of California. Congress voted for a territory of Oregon with restrictions on slavery. There was no decision on California and New Mexico

1849   *Roberts* vs. *City of Boston:* Massachusetts Supreme Court enunciated the doctrine of "separate but equal" educational facilities

1850   Compromise of 1850, provided for admission of California to the Union as a free state, admission of New Mexico and Utah with or without slavery as their constitutions prescribe, a broader Fugitive Slave Act, and the abolition of the slave trade in the District of Columbia

1851   Frederick Douglass and William Lloyd Garrison split on tactics of the abolitionist movement

1852   Publication of *Uncle Tom's Cabin*, a novel by Harriet Beecher Stowe, which attacks the evils of slavery

1854   Kansas-Nebraska Act, provided for the organization of territories of Kansas and Nebraska with or without slavery, and the repeal of the Missouri Compromise of 1820

1857   Supreme Court, in Dred Scott decision, upheld the Fugitive Slave Law and the idea that blacks could never become citizens

1858   Lincoln-Douglas debates, in which Lincoln advocated the continuance of the Fugitive Slave Act, gradual abolition of slavery in the District of Columbia, Congressional prohibition of slavery in the territories, and the gradual extinction of slavery in the United States

1859   John Brown's raid at Harpers Ferry, Va.

           Last slave ship landed shipment of slaves at Mobile Bay, Ala.

1860   Jefferson Davis' Resolutions adopted by Senate, stating that all attacks on slavery violated the Constitution, that the national government should protect slavery in the territories, and that state laws interfering with the recovery of runaway slaves were unconstitutional

1861   Civil War declared

           Navy authorized enlistment of slaves

1862   Congress authorized President Lincoln to accept blacks for military service

Congress declared that the U.S. should cooperate with any state that adopted gradual abolition by paying for the slaves

1863   Emancipation Proclamation signed by Lincoln

1865   Thirteenth Amendment to the Constitution, abolishing slavery in America

Black codes passed in all reconstructed states, almost reenslaving the newly freed blacks

Congress established Freedmen's Bureau to aid refugees and freedmen

Jefferson Davis signed bill authorizing use of slaves as soldiers in the Confederate Army

1866   Civil Rights Bill passed over presidential veto, declaring freedmen to be U.S. citizens

Ku Klux Klan founded to defeat radical reconstruction and establish white supremacy by violence in the South

1868   Fourteenth Amendment, guaranteeing citizenship and equal civil rights to freedmen

1870   Fifteenth Amendment, banning voting discrimination on the "basis of race, color, or previous condition of servitude"

1875   Civil Rights Law, prohibiting discrimination in hotels

Race riots in Mississippi

1877   Compromise of 1877, wherein southern congressmen agreed to the election of Hayes as President if Republicans promised to withdraw federal troops from the South

1879   Exodus of some 50,000 blacks to the North

1881–   Tennessee began modern segregation movement with Jim Crow
1907   railroad car law; Florida, Mississippi, Texas, Louisiana, Alabama, Kentucky, Arkansas, Georgia, South Carolina, North Carolina, Virginia, Maryland, and Oklahoma followed suit

1883	Civil Rights Act of 1875 held unconstitutional

1883   Civil Rights Act of 1875 held unconstitutional

1886   Twenty blacks lynched in Carrollton, Miss.

1890   Mississippi Constitutional Convention began systematic exclusion of blacks from political life in the South, using literacy and "understanding" tests, which were later adopted and embellished by South Carolina, Louisiana, North Carolina, Alabama, Virginia, Georgia, and Oklahoma

1891   Colored Farmers' Alliance organized in twenty states

1896   *Plessy* vs. *Ferguson:* Court upheld doctrine of "separate but equal" as it relates to civil rights of blacks

1904   Formation of the National Liberty Party, an Afro-American national political organization

1908   Race riot, Springfield, Ill., leading to the founding of the NAACP on Feb. 12, 1909, the 100th anniversary of Lincoln's birthday

1915   U.S. Marines' occupation of Haiti until 1934

1916   U.S. occupation of the Dominican Republic until 1924

1917   U.S. purchase of the Virgin Islands

          Ten thousand blacks paraded in New York City, protesting lynching and discrimination

1917–
1918   360,000 Afro-Americans returned from World War I, demanding equal rights and opportunities

1919   Twenty-five major race riots

          National Urban League founded

1920   Development of the Negro Renaissance

Marcus Garvey's black nationalist movement, Universal
Improvement Association, held national convention in Liberty
Hall, Harlem, N.Y.

1923   500,000 blacks migrated to the North

1933   NAACP initiated court attacks on segregation and discrimination
        in education

1941   President Franklin D. Roosevelt established Fair Employment
        Practices Commission to prohibit discrimination in defense
        industries because of race, color, creed, or national origin

1943   Congress of Racial Equality (CORE) organized

1944   War Department abolished segregation on Army posts

        Texas primary elections, which excluded Afro-Americans,
        held unconstitutional by the Supreme Court

1945   New York Fair Employment Law set up

1946   Race riots in Columbia, Tenn.; Athens, Ga.; and Philadelphia,
        Penn.

        Segregated interstate bus travel banned by Supreme Court

        President Truman created the Presidential Committee on Civil
        Rights

1948   President Truman issued ban on discrimination in the armed
        forces

        States' Rights Party founded, with platform based on racial
        segregation; Strom Thurmond of South Carolina nominated
        for President

1950   Gwendolyn Brooks became the first black to win a Pulitzer
        Prize

        Ralph J. Bunche, highest ranking American in U.N. Secretariat
        (1951), awarded Nobel Peace Prize

1953   *Terry* vs. *Adams*: Supreme Court held that segregated primary
        elections violated the Fourteenth Amendment

1954   Supreme Court decision, *Brown* vs. *Board of Education of
        Topeka, Kansas*, ruled racial segregation in public schools
        unconstitutional

1955   Interstate Commerce Commission banned segregation in busses,
        waiting rooms, and travel coaches involved in interstate travel

        Montgomery, Ala., bus boycott commenced after Mrs. Rosa
        Parks was arrested for refusing to 'move to the back of the bus'

1956   Manifesto issued by 100 senators and congressmen, promising
        to use "all lawful means" to overthrow the Brown decision of
        1954

        Supreme Court ordered the University of Alabama to admit its
        first black student

1957   Southern Christian Leadership Conference organized, with the
        Rev. Dr. Martin Luther King, Jr., as president

        Supreme Court ruled Jim Crow busses unconstitutional

        Federal Civil Rights Commission created

        One thousand federal troops sent to Little Rock, Ark., after
        Governor Faubus ordered out the national guard to prevent
        nine black students from attending an all-white high school

        Civil Rights Act of 1957 passed, guaranteeing blacks the right
        to vote

1960   Student Nonviolent Coordinating Committee (SNCC) organized

        "Sit-in" movement began in Greensboro, N.C., against segrega-
        tion at lunch counters

        Black Nationalist leader Elijah Muhammad called for creation
        of a separate state for blacks

        President Eisenhower signed the Civil Rights Act of 1960,
        providing for court enforcement of the right to vote

        24th Amendment, banning the poll tax in federal elections,
        passed; ratified in 1964

1961   Committee on Equal Employment Opportunity established

        CORE began Freedom Rides through the South

        First desegregation in public education in Georgia occurred
        peacefully as two blacks enrolled at Georgia University

1962   Continuation of demonstrations against discrimination in both
        the North and South

        Citizens in large northern cities began suits claiming de facto
        segregation in northern schools

        3000 federal troops sent to University of Mississippi to prevent
        riot over admission of James H. Meredith, first Afro-American
        student

        Executive order issued, banning discrimination in federally
        assisted housing

1963   Rev. Dr. Martin Luther King, Jr., led mass demonstrations in
        Birmingham, Ala., to desegregate the city

        Voter registration drives held in the South

        Medgar W. Evers, a NAACP leader, assassinated in Jackson, Miss.

        March on Washington, D.C.

        Mass demonstrations in Cambridge, Md., for access to public
        accommodations

        School boycotts in Chicago, New York, and other northern
        cities protest de facto segregation

        Alabama's Governor George Wallace carried out his campaign
        pledge to "stand in the schoolhouse door" to prevent integra-
        tion of Alabama's schools

        Bomb killed four black girls attending Sunday School in
        Birmingham, Ala.

1964   Riots in Harlem, Jersey City, Philadelphia, Rochester, and
        Chicago

        Three civil rights workers murdered near Philadelphia, Miss.

        Rev. Dr. Martin Luther King, Jr., awarded Nobel Peace Prize

Civil Rights Act signed by President Johnson, containing strong public accommodations and fair employment sections

New York City bussing program to end de facto segregation instituted

Selma to Montgomery, Ala., marchers met by state troopers

1965   Malcolm X assassinated

President Johnson issued order creating cabinet-level Council on Equal Opportunity

Voting Rights Bill passed

Watts riot, Los Angeles, Calif., leaving 34 dead, 856 injured, and property damage approaching $200 million

Marches on Selma and Montgomery, Ala., led by Rev. Dr. Martin Luther King, Jr., Ralph Bunche, and Ralph D. Abernathy

The Moynihan Report, "The Negro Family: The Case for National Planning," issued

1966   Stokeley Carmichael introduced concept of "Black Power"

James Meredith wounded while leading a protest march in rural Mississippi

Riots in Cleveland and Chicago

Civil Rights bill aimed at ending housing discrimination failed in Congress

President Johnson sponsored White House Conference, "To Fulfill These Rights"

1967   California constitutional amendment, which gave property owners the right to discriminate in the sale and rental of housing, held unconstitutional

Thurgood Marshall became first Afro-American appointed to the United States Supreme Court

Life of the Civil Rights Commission extended five years

Virginia anti-miscegenation law held unconstitutional

Newark riots, lasting five days, left 25 dead, 725 injured, and caused property damage estimated at $15 million

Detroit riots, lasting five days, left 43 dead, 657 injured, and caused extensive property damage

Carl Stokes elected mayor of Cleveland and Richard Hatcher elected mayor of Gary, Ind.; blacks elected to local offices throughout the country

1968   Rev. Dr. Martin Luther King, Jr., assassinated in Memphis, Tenn., April 4

Poor People's March on Washington, D.C.

Three black students killed during demonstrations at Orangeburg, S.C.

Civil Rights Act signed by President Johnson, with anti-riot, open housing, and civil-rights workers protection provisions

Supreme Court held Alabama law requiring segregation of races in prisons and jails unconstitutional

Black Power salute by two black athletes at Olympics (Mexico City)

Alabama's Governor George Wallace ran for President and captured 13.6 percent of the 9.8 million votes cast and 45 electoral votes

Riots and demonstrations in over a hundred cities across the nation

Supreme Court upheld 1866 Civil Rights law barring racial discrimination in the sale or rental of real property

National Advisory Commission on Civil Disorders cites "white racism" as the underlying cause of urban riots

1969   President Nixon issued Executive Order 11478, ordering federal officials to end job discrimination in federal agencies

The Philadelphia Plan to increase minority employment on federally supported construction projects adopted by approximately 50 cities nation-wide

1970	In a confidential memo, Presidential Counselor Daniel P. Moynihan proposed to President Nixon that the issue of race relations could benefit from a period of "benign neglect"
	Black members of the House of Representatives formed a "shadow cabinet"
	Congress extended the Civil Rights Act of 1956 (voting rights) five years
	Black Panther leader Fred Hampton and other party members killed in raid on party headquarters by Chicago police
	Two black students killed by police gunfire during demonstrations at Jackson (Miss.) State College
1971	Supreme Court approved bussing as a means to achieve school integration
	House Committee on Internal Security reported that the Black Panther Party represented no danger to the federal government
	The "shadow cabinet" reorganized as the Congressional Black Caucus
	Congress approved a constitutional amendment lowering the voting age; ratified by states within a few months
1972	Congress approved the Equal Employment Opportunities Enforcement Act
	Equal Rights Amendment passed by Congress, sent to states for ratification
	Anti-bussing forces who are not from the South became a majority in the House of Representatives; President Nixon signed into law a bill prohibiting bussing solely to achieve racial integration
	Major race riot occurred aboard the USS *Kitty Hawk*
	First National Black Political Convention held in Gary, Ind.
	Angela Davis acquitted of conspiracy to kidnap and murder
1973	Maynard Jackson elected mayor of Atlanta, Ga., and Thomas Bradley elected mayor of Los Angeles

Fraternal Order of Elks agreed to admit blacks and other members of minority groups

1974   Supreme Court held that Detroit did not have to develop a comprehensive metropolitan bussing program, encompassing 53 surrounding suburbs, to integrate its predominantly black school system

Serious outbreak of violence, demonstrations, and boycotts followed implementation of bussing program in Boston

Index

191